ALCOHOL AND DRUG ABUSE

A psychosocial and spiritual approach
to prevention

ALCOHOL AND DRUG ABUSE

*A psychosocial and spiritual approach
to prevention*

A-M. Ghadirian, M.D.

GEORGE RONALD
OXFORD

GEORGE RONALD, *Publisher*
Oxford
www.grbooks.com

An updated and revised edition of *In Search of Nirvana*
First published 1985
Revised 1989

ISBN: 978-0-85398-516-7

A catalogue record for this book is available from the British Library

CONTENTS

FOREWORD

Robert L. DuPont, M.D.*

In this wonderful book Dr Ghadirian extends his brilliant career as professor of psychiatry at McGill University by combining it with his deep, personal faith. He brings a fresh perspective on one of the world's biggest, most modern and most challenging epidemics: the use of illegal drugs.

While drug use has been around for more than a thousand years, never before the late 1960s has the world seen entire national – and now global – populations exposed to a wide range of abuse-able drugs used by powerful routes of administration. Previously illegal drug use was limited to certain sections of the population and to one or at the most a very few drugs. Often the routes of administration used were oral rather than the more high-risk routes of administration: smoking, injecting intravenously and snorting. Today the list of abused drugs is so long it is nearly limit-less, the routes of administration ensure an addiction risk unheard of in earlier eras, and the at-risk population is greatly expanded. The highest risk from illegal drugs is concentrated among youth

---

* First Director of the US National Institute on Drug Abuse (NIDA); Clinical Professor of Psychiatry, Georgetown Medical School; President, Institute for Behaviour and Health, Inc. (see www.ibhinc. org); author of *The Selfish Brain – Learning From Addiction*.

and the disadvantaged including the poor and those with mental illnesses. The drug abuse epidemic is as modern as the computer. It has become commonplace to call addiction to drugs a 'brain disease'. The target organ of all drug use is the brain, and within the brain the target of drug users is the normal reward centres. These biological gatekeepers for pleasure are hijacked by drug abuse. The two most urgent public health questions today about this epidemic are first, why has there been a worldwide explosion of drug use in recent decades; and second, what can be done to reverse this deadly trend toward increasing illegal drug use?

With respect to the first question it is clear that many of the most commonly used drugs are old drugs, starting with marijuana, cocaine and heroin which dominate the world drug use scene. It is also clear that whatever the biological risk factors, including genetic risk factors, the brains of humans have not developed a new biology over the past few decades. In other words, if we are to explain the epidemic rise in drug use over this relatively short period of time we cannot explain it by focusing on changes in the most commonly used drugs or changes in human brain biology. The changes in the rate of drug use, the drug abuse epidemic, can only be explained by changes in the environment in which people come into contact with drugs. These changes have been profound because there has been an increasing globalization of drug trafficking and a global shift in attitudes toward more acceptance of illegal drug use and a shift toward seeing illegal drug use itself as less risky than was thought in previous generations. These efforts to normalize illegal drug use have been deeply rooted in modern culture. They have been well-financed by their enthusiastic supporters.

The modern culture that permits, and even promotes, illegal drug use is one that sees much illegal drug use as without negative consequences to the user or the community and that sees the decision to use drugs as a lifestyle choice to be protected. There is a widespread modern attitude that privacy protections extend to illegal drug users protecting them from interference. These values encourage, and are supported by, a moral relativism about illegal drug use seeing it as no more matter of public concern than clothing styles or styles of speech.

The antidote to the poison of these now common attitudes toward illegal drug use begins with the recognition that illegal drug use is not 'victimless' and that the consequences of illegal drug use are not borne only by the drug users. Families, communities and even entire nations are harmed substantially by the so-called personal choice to use illegal drugs. Whether those consequences are crimes or overdoses, whether they are lowered workplace productivity or educational failure, these negative consequences of illegal drug use are universally shared. These serious and widespread public consequences of illegal drug use justify strong public action to curb it. The recognition of these consequences exposes the fallacy of the view that illegal drug use is a purely personal decision.

If the international public health effort to reduce illegal drug use is to succeed it will not be primarily because of efforts to curb the supply of drugs but because of success in reducing the demand for drugs. At its heart the problem of drug use prevention is deeply personal because the decision to use or not to use illegal drugs is deeply personal. One of the most striking effects of illegal drug use that I have seen in my own practice of psychiatry over the past four decades is the spiritual and moral degradation that drug use causes. Drug use causes a bankruptcy of the soul. At the centre of this bankruptcy is dishonesty. That is the central problem in drug addiction. It is not possible to be an honest addict because the people around addicts, those who care about their welfare, want all addicts to stop their drug use. Since addicts do not want to give up either their chemical lovers – their drugs – or their important relationships with the people trying to get them to stop drug use, they lie. They often lie not just about their drug use but about anything at all that will get them what they want when they want it, often heedless of the long-term consequences of their lying for them and for others. The other side of that coin is that when addicts get well the healing is not just physical, it is also spiritual. The hallmark of recovery from addiction is honesty.

The place many addicts get well and the place they go to stay well is to meetings of the 12-step programmes, especially Alcoholics Anonymous and Narcotics Anonymous. These are more than mutual aide organizations or self-help programmes. As one member of these programmes told me years ago, 'Self-help is what got us into this mess you call addiction.' I asked what I should call these life-saving programmes if not mutual aide programmes or self-help programmes. His response shocked me, 'These are God-aide programmes.' They are not, however, religious programmes, but instead they are spiritual programmes based on a respect for a power greater than one's self. Drug abuse prevention and the recovery from drug use both have profoundly spiritual dimensions.

These little known but important facts about illegal drug use are reflected in Dr Ghadirian's book. He zeroes in on the spiritual pathology of addiction. He offers wise counsel in building a strong spiritual defence against addiction. If a person has a reason to live, a reason to choose one activity today instead of another based on something other than selfishness and other than immediate pleasure, that person is powerfully protected against addiction. If a person has no purpose to his or her life other than immediate pleasure then that person is at high risk of drug dependence, since drugs work powerfully in the present to produce brain reward. The process of addiction can be called the pursuit of 'pleasure', although in later stages of addiction the addict is more likely to be seeking relief from distress (much of it induced by drug use) than seeking to find pleasure. Some of the most unhappy people I have known are drug addicts. This is no 'pleasure disease'. Instead drug use is a reckless and destructive corruption of healthy brain biology rooted deeply in a spiritual wasteland.

This book provides a spiritual vaccination against addiction.

March 2007

To all those
who search for meaning and true happiness in life

ACKNOWLEDGEMENTS

This book began its life in 1985 as *In Search of Nirvana* and was updated in 1989. Since then extensive research has been done in the field of substance abuse and its prevention. With the passage of time and the spread of illicit drugs and addiction, the pressing task has been to address preventive education worldwide.

Several individuals have assisted me in this important undertaking and I am grateful to all who offered their views and encouragement. Foremost among them is my dear wife Marilyn to whom I am immensely grateful for her thoughtful recommendations, selfless assistance and valuable review and editing of the manuscript. I am also thankful to our sons, Sina and Nayyer, for their unfailing love and encouragement. I would like to express my thanks to George Ronald and its staff for their assistance, particularly to May Hofman Öjermark for her wise and invaluable suggestions and editing of my work from the first edition to the present. Among others who helped me with technical assistance and useful views were Johanna Okker and Claire Gougeon, to whom I am grateful. I hope that this book will offer new perspectives on this vital subject.

Abdu'l-Missagh Ghadirian
Mont-Royal, Quebec, Canada
May 2007

INTRODUCTION

The pervasive problem of substance abuse and addiction has spread all over the world and created a crisis of apocalyptic proportions in human society. Today, thousands of adults, youth and even children willingly subject their minds and bodies to the non-medical use of drugs and their serious consequences. According to the United Nations *World Drug Report* (2006) about 200 million people of the world or 5 per cent of the global population between the ages of 15 and 64 consumed drugs during the year preceding the publication of the report. The report also indicates that 64 million inhabitants of this planet use opiates, cocaine, and amphetamine-type stimulants.

Aside from the non-medical drugs, consumption of tobacco alone involves more than 1.3 billion of the global population. Tobacco kills one in two long-term tobacco users. Taking all forms of tobacco users, the statistical casualties of cigarette smoking top 4.9 million deaths annually. Tobacco claims 25 times as many lives as illicit drugs abuse. Millions of people including youth are affected by alcohol and methamphetamine also known as 'crystal meth', or ecstasy. Thousands of children are born addicts each year, unaware of their plight and its consequences.

Why do people use drugs? What are drugs a substitute for? Who is most vulnerable to substance abuse? What is the solution?

Different people use illicit drugs for different purposes. Some do it out of curiosity or for pleasure, while others do it to shield themselves from pain, despair or life stress. And for yet others, it is an escape. Cultural attitudes and the availability of drugs play an important role in the expansion of substance abuse. In many industrialized countries, drugs seem to fit perfectly into the lifestyle of the population. The desire for instant gratification, the low frustration tolerance, the competitive lifestyle and anxiety caused by materialism are contributing factors.

Lifestyle drugs are a new generation of prescribed drugs. They have been emerging in response to various needs such as losing weight, growing hair, increasing sexual drive and boosting mood and self-esteem. Although some of these medications are needed for health, in general this new development underlines how much fulfilling our inner needs for well-being has become dependent on outer objects.

The worldwide spread of substance abuse and its heavy toll on the minds and bodies of millions of people reflects a crisis of human identity and at the same time is a search for an enduring solution to this dilemma. In this crisis, what is always at stake is the human mind, that precious and exquisite gift of knowledge which has become a prime target for distortion and destruction. Our body is the physical frame of the inner temple, the inner reality of existence. Whatever happens to this physical frame will have an impact on the development of the inner reality, the human rational soul.

It is ironic that substances of abuse, with all their tragic consequences, are eagerly sought after, paid for and consumed by people who welcome such an enemy to occupy their brains and influence their minds. This raises a critical question about one's relationship to one's true self. I believe that the artificial manipulation of natural emotions, thoughts and consciousness by illicit drugs will have far-reaching effects on the development of human behaviour, mind and character. The use of drugs, whether for 'entertainment', escape or relief, inhibits the natural process of learning that occurs through life's challenges, and thus intellectual and spiritual progress is impeded. In addition, some drugs diminish or interfere with human responsiveness to environmental challenges and stimuli which are essential for personal growth and maturity.

The main focus of this book is primary prevention of substance abuse and addiction. It is also intended to examine the meaning and implications of drug use in society. At present the most effective, enduring and cost-effective solution to the devastating impact of substance abuse is prevention: the large-scale education of people, especially youth and children. Equally important is concentration on the positive side of well-being and the promotion of a healthy and well-balanced lifestyle. The model of primary prevention presented in this book underlines the fact that preventive education should begin at home and in early childhood, when behavioural attitudes toward life and its sanctity begin to develop. The book also explores the role and responsibilities of the individual, family and society in eradicating this scourge of humanity. As the United Nations former Secretary-General Javier Pérez de Cuéllar (1985) stated:

> Drug abuse presents as destructive a threat to this and coming generations as the plagues which swept many parts of the world in earlier centuries. Unless controlled, its effect will be more insidious and devastating . . . the moment has arrived for the international community to expand its efforts in a global undertaking to meet this peril.

For practical purposes in this book, the word 'substance' is used to denote alcohol and all other types of abused drugs. The terms 'drug use' and 'substance abuse' are used interchangeably to refer to non-medical and illicit drug use of any kind, including drug addiction. Addiction or dependency is a compulsive alcohol or drug-taking behaviour which usually results in development of tolerance and withdrawal symptoms. The addict continues this out-of-control behaviour despite knowledge of the consequences. The expressions 'abuse' and 'recreational use' refer to non-medical use of substances which will cause psychological or physiological symptoms.

Since it was first published in 1985, *In Search of Nirvana* has become increasingly known and has been disseminated in many parts of the world. It has been translated and published in several languages including Spanish, Italian, Russian, Portuguese, Persian and partially in French. It is in the process of being translated and published in Chinese. This third edition has been thoroughly revised and updated; the new title reflects a growing realization in the world of the devastating effects of drug abuse and of the spiritual vacuum it attempts – unsuccessfully – to fill.

1

A SHORT HISTORY OF DRUG USE

From time immemorial man has longed to discover the secret of eternal life and has searched for ways to dispel sorrow and achieve lasting joy. Over the centuries, an array of herbs and medicines which are believed to do this have been found and venerated in various cultures. Many of these substances were used in tribal festivities and religious rites to evoke ecstasy or bring on a state of trance. Depending on the quantity and potency of the substance, users experienced a selective or total dissociation from reality and, at times, suffered seizures and unconsciousness. In some cultures, the consumers of these substances would perform ritualistic dances and rhythmic movements which accelerated as their excitement reached its peak. Such individuals were valued because it was believed that at the height of their ecstasy they could communicate with spirits or supernatural powers to obtain cures or bring about prosperity.

Mood and mind-altering drugs are derived from both natural and synthetic sources. Plants have provided man with natural sources of drugs for thousands of years. Some of the drugs prepared from these are: opium (from the *Papaversom-niferum* plant), marijuana and hashish (from *Cannabis sativa),* cocaine (from the coca plant), mescaline (from the mescal cactus) and alcohol (which can be made from a variety of grains, vegetables and fruits).

Cocaine is the alkaloid and active ingredient contained in the leaves of the coca plant. This plant grows on the eastern slopes of the Andes, particularly in Peru and Bolivia. The coca leaf was central to the culture of South American Indians. Coca, which means 'tree' comes from the language of the Aymara Indians. The Incas regarded the coca leaves, which were burned or chewed in religious ceremonies, as sacred (UNDCP1997, p. 34). Long before the 1880s when European physicians began to study the therapeutic effects of coca, the Indians used it to treat various ailments including altitude sickness and toothache. It was also used to reduce appetite, relieve hunger and thirst, and to ease the burden of hard manual work. This traditional knowledge was later exploited by the Spaniards in Latin America, who used it to induce Native American workers to labour for long hours (ibid.).

The first medical application of cocaine was in 1884 as a local anaesthetic in eye surgery and also in the treatment of morphine and alcohol addiction. The medical use of cocaine as a local anaesthetic was subsequently expanded to dentistry and many other fields of surgery until better synthetic substitutes were found (Kalant 1986, p. 9). However, its use as a treatment for morphine and alcohol addiction eventually led to a spreading misuse and self-administration of the substance. Initially it was administered through subcutaneous injection, but by the turn of the century the practice of sniffing cocaine spread rapidly, reaching its peak after the First World War. From then on for 50 years the use of cocaine remained very limited. In the 1970s, however, its popularity began to rise, especially among multiple drug users (ibid.). The consumption of crack, a purer, more concentrated and cheaper form of cocaine, and extremely addictive, rose dramatically in the 1980s, especially in the urban areas of the United States. It has since spread to all parts of the industrialized world.

Marijuana is prepared from the dried flowery tops and leaves of the hemp plant while **hashish** is a concentrated resin form of this plant. Hashish is usually a stronger component and has traditionally been more commonly used in the East, while marijuana is more frequently used in the West. The potency of any cannabis preparation depends on the amount of tetrahydrocannabinol (THC) its resin contains.

Hashish has been used in India and Egypt since prehistoric times. Pre-Christian Hindus regarded cannabis as a holy plant that played an important role in their religious activities. In Sanskrit literature it is referred to as 'the food of gods' (Nahas 1981, p. 7). Towards the end of the eleventh century, some of the followers of an oriental sect led by Hasan-i-Sabbah, 'the Old Man of the Mountain' in northern Persia, used hashish for special purposes. Those who were to attempt dangerous missions would first partake of hashish and would then be brought to a beautiful garden which they were told was a reflection of the eternal paradise they were destined to enter upon completion of their mission.

> For the sake of the glimpse of paradise which the drug afforded, his fanatical henchmen would gladly ride across the desert to Basra or Baghdad, there stealthily to murder certain individuals of whom Hassan happened to disapprove. For this reason the furtive secret political murderer is known even today as an 'assassin' (hashishin), a name supposedly derived from that of the drug (De Ropp 1976, p. 52).

In some parts of Jamaica, marijuana (ganja) used to be provided to labourers and farmers in the belief that it gave them more energy and made them work harder (Cohen 1981a, p. 1). Hence, ganja breaks were taken like North American and European coffee breaks. Many farmers in South and Central America began growing marijuana and coca rather than traditional food crops because of the greatly increased profit.

According to the Sumerian Tablets, the use of **opium** originated in the eastern Mediterranean region over 5,000 years ago and spread to Persia, Egypt, China and Europe.

> The ancient Sumerians, who used opium for a thousand years before Christ, identified the poppy from which this drug is extracted with a symbolic lettering meaning 'joy'. While opium derivatives and cannabis preparations were used in the East and Far East, in the new world, tobacco and hallucinogenic cacti were

used in prehistoric times. These confections were either sniffed or ingested and later inhaled (UN 1982, p. 8).

In Asia opium was used for centuries for aches and pains and to overcome stress and bereavement. Warriors would use it as a painkiller for battle wounds and they also thought opium would enhance their strength and sexual potency (UNDCP 1997, p. 35).

Morphine was identified as an alkaloid of opium in 1803. In 1890, **heroin** was synthesized and by the turn of the century was available for the treatment of morphine addiction. It soon proved itself to be, however, a stronger addicting agent than morphine.

The hallucinogen **psilocybin** of southern Mexico was consumed in religious rites long before the Aztec civilization flourished. The **peyote** (or peyotl) cactus plant *(Lophophora Williamsii)* has been used by the Indians of Mexico to overcome alcoholism. According to Indian legends, peyote is of 'divine origin'. The word 'peyotl' is said to mean 'to stir' or 'to stimulate'. It has been known in Mexico since the 17th century; its earliest application was in traditional medicine as well as in certain tribal rites (ibid. p. 34).

The illicit use of **narcotics** has also been common for centuries. During the American Civil War in the 1860s, the use of morphine became widespread for the first time. Following each of the World Wars, many veterans and disillusioned survivors sought refuge and comfort in the use of these habit-forming substances in order to obliterate their painful memories.

In 1943 the hallucinogenic drug **LSD** (lysergic acid diethyla-mide) was discovered by a chemist who accidentally swallowed a dose of this substance. The use of this and other hallucinogenic drugs, also known as **psychedelics,** in the 1960s brought on a wave of search and adventure into the deeper layers of consciousness, as well as popular excursions into the world of unreality. These substances alter the form of consciousness without diminishing alertness. Experiments in mind expansion spread from the streets into universities and psychological laboratories.

In some developing countries in Africa, Southern Asia and the Middle East, the use of cannabis is widespread both among the lower socio-economic and affluent upper-class groups. It has a 'socially sanctioned limited use' for ceremonial purposes as well as 'socially unsanctioned regular use' (Alcoholism and Drug Addiction Research Foundation 1981, p. 34). Exploring the socio-cultural meaning of such cannabis use, some researchers indicated that in India, for example, the great majority of Hindus participate in the ceremonial use of cannabis in special events such as the festival of Shiva. Regular self-administration of it occurs only in a small proportion of the Hindu population (ibid.). In North America and Europe the pattern of use is different and the quantity of drug consumption is often excessive.

In recent years synthetic substances known as 'designer drugs' have been manufactured in clandestine chemistry laboratories and have been added to the list of deadly drugs which are abused. They have a more potent effect than cocaine, cost less and are hardly detected in the usual drug test. Their existence has added to the already mounting concern regarding the dangers of drug abuse.

Alcohol and tobacco, although not classified as illicit drugs, are, however, implicated in substance abuse. Alcohol in particular, and also marijuana, are viewed as 'gateway drugs' since the majority of drug users, particularly in the western hemisphere, begin their substance abuse initially through experiences with alcohol, marijuana, or tobacco consumption.

Ethyl alcohol or **ethanol** is formed through fermentation of various fruit juices and cereals. The history of wine-making goes back to the early Egyptians. Tablets belonging to the ancient Babylonians indicate that they knew about the process of brewing beer from malted barley. The initial use of alcohol was in the preservation of food – its influence on the mind and its medicinal effects were discovered later. Brewing and wine-making became very important during the Middle Ages because wine was used to celebrate the sacrament of the Mass. During the Renaissance period the manufacture of alcoholic beverages became an important industry.

The problem of alcoholism has been found only rarely among the Chinese people and the Jews. On the other hand, it occurs

9

more commonly among the Irish and the American Indians. Recent research studies suggest that genetic predisposition can partly explain this difference. Oriental people, particularly the Chinese, have biological defences which can be explained by the presence of a higher level of acetaldehyde in their blood following drinking. Acetaldehyde, a by-product of the breakdown of alcohol in the body, causes a strong, unpleasant flushing response which presumably protects them from excessive drinking. Such biological defences are thought to be lower in Irish people and American Indians and therefore they can more easily indulge in drinking and develop alcoholism (Prince 1982).

Tobacco contains **nicotine** which stimulates the heart, nervous system and other organs. The American Indians smoked tobacco in pipes long before the American continent was discovered in 1492. Christopher Columbus brought tobacco seeds back to Europe and farmers began to cultivate this plant as a medicine, believing it would help people to relax. At the beginning of the 20th century tobacco was consumed mostly by the chewing of tobacco leaf. However, this practice gave rise to a greater number of patients who developed cancer of the tongue and mouth. The practice of chewing tobacco began to decrease during the 1920s, partly because spitting was found to be associated with the spread of tuberculosis which at that time had no cure. Gradually chewing tobacco disappeared and cigarette smoking became the fashion (Stuart Houston 1986). In recent years the tobacco plant has ranked as an important crop in more than 60 countries, with China leading the world in tobacco production.

Another group of substances easily abused is the **psycho-tropic medications.** These include sedatives and hypnotics, barbiturates and non-barbiturate medications as well as tranquillizers such as benzodiazepines. Most of these substances are highly addictive and are used extensively for a wide range of medical and psychological problems ranging from the management of epilepsy to the alleviation of anxiety. Each year it is estimated that over 100 million prescriptions are written based on this group of drugs (Inaba et al. 1977, p. 15). The tranquillizing and relaxing effects of these substances have been exploited and abused by a large number of adolescents and adults as a means of overcoming psychological conflicts or to obtain pleasure.

Substance abuse: An international perspective

In 1987 the Commission on Narcotic Drugs of the United Nations expressed grave concern over the spread of drug problems throughout the world. In some countries, they said, the problem had reached epidemic proportions. Heroin and cocaine abuse had escalated noticeably. Although in some countries the number of new cases had stabilized and was even decreasing, the total number of abusers was still very high.

A new cause for concern was the appearance of 'designer drugs' – analogues of controlled drugs whose structures had been changed to circumvent their control but whose effects were similar to, or even stronger than, those of the original. The use of such substances was associated with increased morbidity and mortality (UN 1987).

Problems associated with drug abuse which included 'personal and social dysfunction, crime, accidents, impairment of health and death (predominantly among young people)' and AIDS (Acquired Immune Deficiency Syndrome) caused by the use of unsterilized needles had been added to problems of drug abuse itself. Also, drug use in the workplace and the impairment of professional functioning caused special concern.

Noticeable trends included earlier first drug use (pre-adolescents), a growing proportion of female drug users, frequent use of volatile solvents, cocaine and heroin, and the spread of abuse to all strata of human society. The most popularly abused drugs were cocaine, often inhaled in the form of 'crack', cannabis which 'continued to be the most widely abused illicit drug in most regions' and heroin, which had spread to African countries and constituted a serious problem in most parts of the world.

With regard to other substances, the Commission revealed (ibid.),

11

Abuse of amphetamine-type stimulants was reported from all regions (of the world). Such abuse had increased in a number of countries. Benzodiazepines, minor tranquillizers, barbiturates and non-barbiturate sedative-hypnotics were abused worldwide. The abuse of lysergic acid diethylamide (LSD) appeared to be declining, but it was still a problem in some countries. Phencyclidine (PCP) continued to be abused in North America, but only sporadically elsewhere. Natural hallucinogens, particularly mushrooms, were increasingly abused in several countries. An increasing abuse of volatile solvents, such as glue and petrol, by young adolescents and children was becoming a difficult problem in all regions, particularly from the point of view of control, since solvents were readily available in most countries.

2

ALCOHOL AND DRUG ABUSE: GLOBAL PREVALENCE

Nearly two decades after the Commission's report, the 2006 Annual Report of the United Nation's Office of Drugs and Crime (UNODC) revealed that 5 per cent of the world's population – that is, 200 million people aged 15–64 – had used illicit drugs at least once in the last 12 months (UNODC 2006, p. 9). This figure is 15 million people higher than 2004. However, with respect to licit drugs, it has been estimated that about 50 per cent of the adult population of the world use alcohol while 30 per cent use tobacco (UNODC 2005, p. 5).

Cannabis

Cannabis is the most commonly used illicit drug, consumed by 160 million people or 4 per cent of the world population aged 15–64. Its use, either in the form of herbal cannabis or cannabis resin, is most prevalent in the islands of the Pacific (Oceania) followed by North America and Africa and its consumption in the world is increasing (ibid. p. 93). This increase has been noticeable among students of 15–16 years of age in Europe.

Cocaine

Close to 14 million people use cocaine (ibid. p. 5), a highly prevalent drug in the Americas. According to UNODC, more than 900,000 people were treated for cocaine dependence in 2003 and 90 per cent of them came from the Americas. Only 7 per cent of all cocaine users are currently in treatment and five out of every 10,000 cocaine users die as a result of it each year (ibid. p. 76).

The addictive strength and risk of death in those who use cocaine ranks second only to heroin. Two-thirds of the 14 million cocaine users worldwide live in the Americas. The United States continues to be the largest cocaine market of the world followed by European countries, especially Spain and England (ibid.). It is believed, however, that after years of increase, cocaine use has levelled out in many parts of the world. According to the most recent *World Drug Report*, cocaine use is perceived to be declining slightly (UNODC 2006, p. 9), but while use has decreased in the Americas, consumption has increased in Europe (ibid. pp. 97–98).

Opiates

Before the International Opium Commission was convened in Shanghai, China in 1909, the world production of opium was estimated to have been at least 30,000 metric tons. A hundred years later world production has decreased to about 5,000 metric tons (ibid. p. 7). This last figure includes 400 metric tons of licit opium (for medical use) and the rest for illicit use. On the other hand, the world population has grown from 1.65 billion in 1900 to 6.4 billion at present. Opium production is thus 80 per cent less in a world population three times larger (ibid).

The number of opiate users is estimated to be about 16 million people. There has been an increase, mainly in Asia. Of these 16 million of the world's population who abuse opiates (opium, morphine and heroin) 10.6 million abuse heroin which continues to be the main challenge of global drug abuse. It is estimated that over 60 per cent of drug-related treatment demand in Europe and Asia arises from opiate abuse. Worldwide, only 78 out of 1,000

14

of opiate dependents are in treatment. The mortality caused by opiate abuse is higher than any other kind of drug abuse (UNODC 2005, p. 56). Over 50 per cent of the world's total opiate abusers live in Asia, which is a major producer and trafficker of opiates in the world. Therefore, some Asian countries with the highest level of opiate abuse are those along the routes where drugs are trafficked such as Afghanistan, Iran and Kyrgyzstan (ibid. p. 45). Countries reporting the largest total opiate seizures in 2003 were Pakistan and Iran (31 per cent and 24 per cent of global opiate seizures respectively) (ibid. p. 48). A significant number of people in countries neighbouring Afghanistan are affected by opiate dependency. However, the highest regional prevalence rate of opiates is reported in Europe, especially Eastern Europe (notably the Russian Federation). Heroin abuse in the Americas is concentrated in the United States (ibid. p. 56).

The worldwide level of consumption of ATS, cocaine and opium has remained largely stable in the past three years. The global rate of substance abuse worldwide for 2006 remained the same as in the preceding year (200 million or 5 per cent of the world population). Although there have been some changes in the estimates of drug users in recent years, at the global level the estimate does not seem to have changed; increases in some countries were offset by declines in others. It should also be noted that of the 5 per cent of the population (ages 15–64) who consume illicit drugs at least once a year (annual prevalence), only approximately half of them (2.7 per cent of the same age population) use drugs regularly (that is, at least once a month) (UNODC 2006, p. 8).

Synthetic drugs

Not all illicit drugs are derived from plants or plant products. The use of synthetic or designer drugs is on the rise and these are more easily available. The advantages of synthetic drugs are that they can be produced anywhere and are easily distributed. Thus, they have taken an increasingly important place in the market for illicit substances. The growth of illicit production and trafficking of synthetic stimulants has surpassed that of cocaine and heroin (ibid.

15

vol. 1, p. 38). The principal synthetic drugs manufactured clandestinely are amphetamine-type stimulants (ATS), which include the widely abused amphetamines and methamphetamines as well as the more recently popularized methylenedioxymethamphetamine (MDMA) known as ecstasy (the 'love drug') and methcathione (ibid. p. 19). The name 'ecstasy' refers to a series of designer drugs with slightly different molecular compounds. Thus traffickers can circumvent controls by slightly modifying the formula and creating new drugs with similar effects which are not yet targeted by the law (PEDDRO 1998, pp. 8–9).

ATS and the related substance ecstasy claim a total of 34 million users worldwide between the ages of 15 and 64 – 26 million (0.6 per cent of the world's population) for ATS and 8 million for ecstasy (UNODC 2005, p. 5). Although these figures for drug users vary from year to year, especially in South-East Asia and North America, nevertheless the extent of their use is alarming. Almost two-thirds of the amphetamine and methamphetamine users of the world live in Asia, especially in East and South-East Asia (ibid. p. 112). In Europe, amphetamine use is more common, while in Asia methamphetamine use dominates that of other ATS drugs (ibid.). Ecstasy, on the other hand, is more commonly used in Europe and North America (ibid.), although the use of ecstasy in Oceania has been reported to be on the rise and is higher than in any other region of the world.

The use of ATS was responsible in 2005 for treatment admissions of 16 per cent of patients in Asia, 13 per cent in Oceania, 12 per cent in America and 9 per cent in Europe.

The synthetic drug explosion is considered to have really begun in the mid-1980s (PEDDRO 1998, pp. 5–7). At first it was connected with the emergence of a new subculture in the West: the rave phenomenon. The spread of ecstasy associated with techno music was stunning (ibid.). By the late 1990s, the three most consumed drugs in the United Kingdom were reported to be, in order, cannabis derivatives, amphetamines and ecstasy (ibid. p. 5). The consumption of ecstasy is expanding very quickly, due to its ease of production and the growth of the rave movement (ibid. pp. 8–9). The staggering number of 200 million of the world's population as consumers of illicit drugs, together with the much higher number of those who are dependent on so-called licit drugs such as tobacco and alcohol, reflect a huge population which is engaged in self-destructive behaviour. This has created a global market where the retail price of illicit drugs is estimated to be US$320 billion dollars per year. 'This is not a small enemy against which we struggle,' stated Antonio Maria Costa, Executive Director of UNODC, 'it is a monster. With such an enormous amount of capital at its disposal, it is bound to be an extremely tenacious one' (UNODC 2005, p. 2).

The *World Drug Report* 2005 published a table reflecting the extent of drug use by number and percentage of the affected population of the world (Table 1). Figure 1 illustrates the steady increase of consumption of the four most common substances of abuse, namely cannabis, ATS, cocaine and opiates for the 10-year period 1993–2003.

Table 1
Extent of drug use (annual prevalence*)

estimates 2003/04 (or latest year available)

	All illicit drugs	Cannabis	Amphetamine-type stimulants		Cocaine	Opiates	of which heroin
			Amphetamines	Ecstasy			
(million people)	200	160.9	26.2	7.9	13.7	15.9	10.6
in % of global population age 15–64	5.0%	4.0%	0.6%	0.2%	0.3%	0.4%	0.23%

* Annual prevalence is a measure of the number/percentage of people who have consumed an illicit drug at least once in the 12-month period preceding the assessment. Please note that the figures in Table 1 do not add up to a total of 200 million because some users consume more than one drug. This also applies to the percentages in the table.

Sources: UNODC 2005, based on Annual Reports Questionnaire data, National Reports, UNODC estimates. Reprinted with permission.

Figure 1
Global drug consumption 1993 to 2003

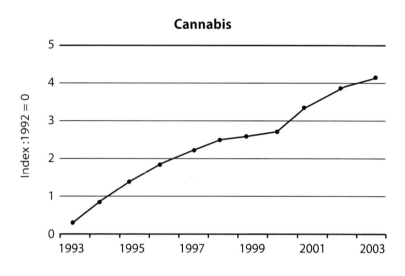

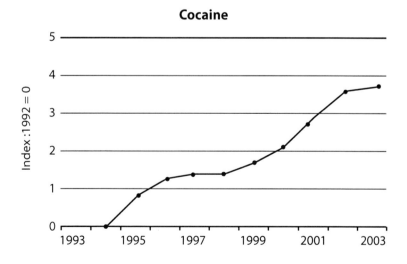

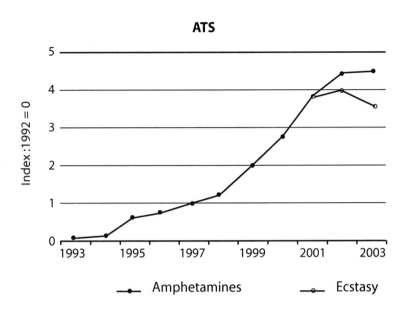

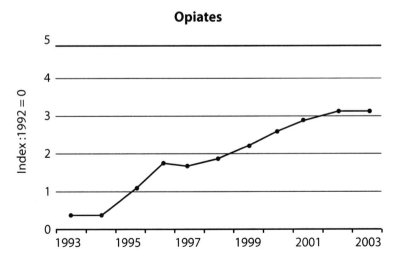

Source: UNODC 2005, p. 7, based on Annual Reports Questionnaire data. Reprinted with permission.

Alcohol: Global consumption

In recent years the global consumption of alcohol has increased. According to the World Health Organization (WHO) (*Globe* 2002, p. 3), most or all of this increase occurred in developing countries. Alcohol caused 1.8 million deaths throughout the world and this number is equal to 4 per cent of the global disease problem. The highest proportion of this tragedy has been in the Americas and Europe. It is estimated that alcohol causes between 20–30 per cent of liver disease, oesophageal cancer, epilepsy, motor vehicle accidents, homicides and other intentional injuries around the world (ibid.). One in four European men and one in ten European women consume alcohol at levels considered harmful and dangerous for health (ibid.). Each year 1.8 million lives or 5,000 lives per day are lost from alcohol consumption around the world. These losses would be preventable, if there was a plan of action and the will to implement it (*Globe* 2006a, p. 11).

In the **United States** approximately 70 million people are affected by alcohol problems either directly (15.4 million alcoholics) or indirectly (56 million) as a result of their dependency on those who are alcoholics (APA 1994, p. 3). Although alcohol and tobacco are considered as drugs, they are not illicit.

Young people between the ages of 12 and 24 number 1.3 billion and that is the largest cohort in history. On average, they are more educated and healthier than past generations. Yet the proportion of young people who report alcohol consumption generally exceeds 60 per cent. Of this, 10–30 per cent are involved in binge drinking. In the United Kingdom, youth aged 16–24 are the heaviest drinkers in the population and are the least likely to abstain from alcohol consumption (*Globe* 2006b, p. 18).

In European countries, drinking alcohol among young people has been on the rise in recent years. The ESPAD Report 2003 on alcohol and drug use among students in 35 European countries revealed continued disturbing trends among youth of school age. The report (*Globe* 2004a, p. 19) states that in two-thirds of those countries (northern and western Europe) almost 90 per cent have drunk alcohol at least once. The highest number reporting use of alcohol 40

20

times or more include Denmark, Austria, the Czech Republic, the Netherlands and the United Kingdom (43–50 per cent). More boys than girls consumed large amounts of alcohol, although in some of these countries the gender distribution is almost equal (ibid.)

The frequency of 'binge drinking' (having 5 or more drinks in a row) has been the highest among the youth of the following European countries: Denmark, Ireland, the Isle of Man, Malta, the Netherlands, Norway, Poland and the United Kingdom (24–32 per cent) (ibid. p. 2).

In **Brazil**, annual per capita alcohol consumption is estimated to be 8.5 litres. Alcohol use may begin as early as 10 years of age in both sexes. A study based on female alcohol dependants presenting for treatment indicated that women begin to drink on average by the age of 18, start abusing alcohol by the age of 31 (later than men) but have fewer years of problem drinking before coming to the treatment centre (8 years for women, 11 years for men). One-third of alcohol-dependent women had attempted suicide as compared to 13 per cent of males (WHO 1993).

In **China**, alcohol consumption increased 20-fold between 1952 and 1990, but although it continues to grow it is still relatively low when compared with western countries and Japan. In the past, those in the lowest economic status had the highest rate of alcohol dependence. But this trend is changing (ibid.).

Tobacco

The use of licit psychoactive substances is a matter for grave concern. Tobacco, an addictive substance, is a case in point. According to the World Health Organization (WHO), about 28 per cent of the world's adult population is estimated to use tobacco. This figure is much higher than the 5 per cent of people, reported above, who use illicit drugs (UNODC 2006, p. 8). Although the addictive power of tobacco is less than some other substances of abuse, its medically adverse effects are far more serious and its availability is worldwide.

It is estimated that currently almost 1.3 billion of the world's peoples smoke tobacco, the majority in developing countries.

Tobacco is addictive and kills one in two long-term users – 4.9 million each year. According to WHO, tobacco use is responsible for more deaths worldwide than any other risk factor except high blood pressure (Esson 2004, p. 13). One hundred million deaths were attributed to tobacco during the 20th century, most of them occurring in developed countries. If the current patterns of consumption continue, it is expected that one billion deaths due to tobacco use will occur in the 21st century, but mostly in developing countries. The majority of tobacco companies have expanded their influence into developing countries in South America, Asia, Eastern Europe and Africa (ibid.).

According to WHO, the consumption of tobacco has reached a global epidemic level. It is deadly in any form or design. Asia, Australia and the Far East are by far the largest consumers, followed by the Americas, Eastern Europe, the former Soviet economies and Western Europe (www.who.int/tobacco/statistics/tobacco_atlas/en/). WHO has also identified the following top five countries as having the highest consumption of tobacco: China, United States, Japan, Russia and Indonesia (in that order).

China has become the world's largest cigarette producer (over 1.6 trillion cigarettes every year) and cigarette consumption there increased about 13 times between 1952 and 1990. The population increased 3 times in the same period. According to the World Health Organization (2003) there are more than 320 million smokers in China and each year 3 million smokers are added. Over 60 per cent of men and 4 per cent of women over the age of 15 smoke tobacco. But China also pays a terrible price for tobacco consumption. About 700,000 Chinese die each year from tobacco-related diseases. Based on an estimation by health experts, this rate will hit 2.5 million by 2025. China has the highest tobacco-related mortality rate in the world.

Some tobacco manufacturers and companies in China and other countries actually urge people to smoke, saying it is good for their health. Websites of some of the tobacco manufacturers have a list of what they call the 'health benefits' of smoking! (WHO 2003). In recent years, the Chinese government has launched anti-smoking campaigns, restricted cigarette advertising and banned smoking in public places which if successful could save millions of lives (ibid.).

Substance Abuse Across Cultures and Societies

Cultural values and traditional beliefs reflect not only the diversity of the people of a nation but also their attitudes toward the age-long quest for attaining peace and tranquillity. With the rapid progress of communication and the availability and spread of substance abuse, pleasure-seeking behaviour has deeply affected people's lifestyles.

European Union. A report issued by the European Monitoring Centre for Drugs and Drug Addiction in 1999 states that one in five 15-year-olds has tried cannabis. More specifically, 40 per cent of people between the ages of 16 and 34 living in England and Wales, Spain, Ireland and Denmark, have used this drug at least once. England and Wales also have the highest percentage of consumption of the drugs ecstasy, LSD and amphetamines.

Drug abuse is increasing and is most prevalent in Britain, Italy and Luxembourg. In Europe about 20 people die of it every day. The highest rates of death are in Greece and Ireland. Moreover, up to 5 per cent of European young adults have taken cocaine at least once, with the highest rates in Spain and France.

On the bright side, it appears that use of marijuana has become stable or even perhaps decreased in some European countries. Furthermore, the drug-related HIV-infected rate among intravenous users is only 1 per cent in England and Wales, compared to 32 per cent in Spain (*Globe* 1999b, p. 10).

In **Hanoi, Viet Nam**, opium use was found to be the most common form of drug abuse (Power 1996, p. 37). Illicit drugs were obtained in 'shooting galleries' in private residences. The ratio of females to males among the opium injectors surveyed was 1:30 and the age of participants in the survey ranged from 19 to 63 (average 31.4 years). Most of the male injectors raised money for drugs through legal and illegal activities while most of the females were sex workers (ibid. p. 39). The 'shooting galleries' were operated by drug dealers who also controlled the use of syringes. The vast majority of injectors shared the syringe with others, often with those they didn't even know. Moreover, in the 'shooting galleries' most of the injectors would draw the opium solution from a shared 'pot'. The solution would come from different preparations including from the black residue of opium smoke ('black water') which was processed for injection. In such a poor hygienic situation, with shared solution and shared needles, the risk of spread of diseases such as infection from HIV was evidently serious.

In **Ethiopia,** 45 per cent of respondents who had ever used addictive substances had begun doing so before the age of 15. Leading factors in substance abuse in the order of importance (Selassie and Gebre 1996, p. 55) were: 1) easy availability; 2) ignorance of the harmful effects of these substances; 3) desire for adventure; 4) peer pressure; 5) boredom and depression; 6) belief that substance abuse would enhance mental alertness and clarity of thought; 7) fulfilment of religious ritual and requirements.

In this study, it was noted that street children abused substances so that they could cope with the frustration, hardship, and boredom associated with street life. For unemployed people, substance abuse provided a pastime and an outlet for their frustration (Selassie and Gebre, 1996, p. 58). The most frequently used substances were **khat** (*Catha edulis*), alcohol, tobacco and cannabis. Khat is available and consumed everywhere in the country and is offered to visitors as an expression of hospitality (ibid. p. 56). Students use khat assuming that it will sharpen their mind and their senses while they prepare for important exams. In some business meetings, khat is chewed while major decisions are being made. Khat is also valued as a sport commodity. The consumption of alcohol and tobacco has also been increasing at an alarming rate. The type of alcohol consumed is perceived as an indication of a person's social status or visibility (ibid. p. 59).

In **Kenya,** according to Mwenesi (1996, p. 65), a senior research scientist of that country, the 'traditional cultural values and discipline of African society prescribed the circumstances in which drugs and intoxicants could be obtained, used and consumed . . . Drinking alcohol was generally the prerogative of the elders – more often than not, of the male elder.' In a study involving 97 health workers and a large number of substance abusers it was found that street children progress from tobacco to gasoline, then glue, and finally to cannabis or khat. However, adults will abuse gasoline and glue when nothing else is available. As in Ethiopia, khat has taken hold, to varying degrees, in the entire country and cannabis use is also widespread (ibid. p. 71).

The following are reasons given for drug abuse (in order of significance): 1) to cope with problems; 2) to feel good; 3) to kill boredom; 4) to gain strength and courage; 5) to belong.

Students use khat for their studies. 'Most of us take khat to remain awake. We all feel we are gaining more, but it leaves one very tired, so then we take Toche 5 (valium) to be able to sleep' (ibid. p. 72). Because of a high level of tolerance, drug abuse has become the order of the day in institutions of higher learning.

As to why street people should take drugs as a crutch, both adults and children gave a graphic explanation: drugs were not a problem but a solution. They reported that their main problems were food, shelter, harassment and disease. 'We abuse drugs to be able to cope with street life. Hunger and cold are specially bad. All of us on the street use drugs. If you refuse, you will starve. There is no mother to go to. Our money is for food and drugs' (ibid. pp. 72, 73).

The traditional method of using drugs is through smoking, chewing, sniffing, inhaling and drinking. Injecting drugs is less common. Traffickers and dealers have learned sophisticated ways of drug transportation. Cannabis poses a major problem for drug traffickers because it is bulky and has a strong smell, so it is transported in loads of fish or while still green, in bundles of vegetables (ibid. p. 73).

In **Cameroon** illicit drugs were traditionally used in cultural rites, and their use then spread to general celebrations. A secret society of Bayangi, an ethnic group, used a mixture of herbs and fruits to concoct *ewimbwe*, which enabled them to recognize 150 'signs'. Another common traditional use of drugs was for treating human disease.

Cannabis had a special place in the traditional doctor's practice. They used certain illnesses to evoke spirits; at other times patients were washed with mixtures containing cannabis to drive away evil spirits. Cannabis was used for sexual purposes or was added to body lotions for patients, and was used to embalm corpses (Wansi 1996, pp. 85–86). Cannabis, amphetamines, cocaine, solvents and benzodiazepines now account for 91 per cent of drug abuse in Cameroon (ibid.).

In a study of the population, the reasons given by the respondents for drug consumption fell into three groups. The reasons of the first group were psychosocial. For example, drug abuse was believed to provide stimulation to enhance courage, to gain social approval, to increase sexual desire, and to enable one to forget problems. The second group gave 'economic reasons': some people abuse drugs because of unemployment, boredom or in response to an advertisement. The third group gave therapeutic reasons such as belief that cannabis has supernatural effects and could protect its users against witchcraft and could increase their chances of success (ibid. p. 83).

In the past, psychotropic substances were used in traditional dances and rituals, especially by older generations. But now cannabis is used by young adults and even children to get high and to muster courage. In most traditional events alcohol was offered, as well as tree bark, roots, or other stimulants such as cola nuts. In addition, there is a belief that drinking alcoholic beverages and smoking are signs of emancipation and of being fashionable.

In **Israel** in 2002, a dairy company marketed a milk beverage called Xtramood with 2 per cent alcohol content. It was promoted as 'the first alcoholic milk beverage in the world produced by a dairy' and was expected to bring in a million dollars in sales until the Ministry of Health ordered its removal (Weiss 2002, p. 20).

In **Brazil** between 35 per cent and 41 per cent of over 150 million habitants are under 15 years of age. There are some 36 million destitute children in the country, nearly half of whom are under 19 years of age. It is further estimated that 7 million have been abandoned by their families or run away from home. The problem of drug abuse in Brazil is worse among the poor. High-risk populations include street children, children and adolescents not attending school and the destitute.

Surveys on drug use by students in 10 metropolitan cities in Brazil showed an increase in reported lifetime and frequent drug use, especially among the youngest males (10–12 years old). While male children are more likely to use cannabis, solvents and cocaine, females prefer anxiolytics and amphetamines. The worsening standard of living, the continuing economic crises, and the lack of systematic educational programmes may be related to increased drug use as a way to escape from reality. Only in the city of Brasilia was there a decrease in drug use; this occurred only among women and the city has good institutions for the prevention and treatment of drug abuse.

Epidemiological studies revealed that the one-year prevalence of psychotropic drug abuse in Sao Paulo was 122 per 1,000 inhabitants (7.6% males and 16.3% females). Consumption increased with age and the higher the standard of living, the higher the reported use (WHO 1993, pp. 59–80).

Indigenous peoples and substance abuse

Indigenous peoples in many parts of the world have been experiencing a serious erosion of their way of life. While in their traditional cultures they were not exposed to the harmful effects of alcohol and mind-altering drugs, in recent times they have not only lost their traditions, but have also been oppressed, their children facing a bleak and uncertain future. Substances of abuse such as alcohol have had a devastating effect on Australian, Native American and other indigenous peoples, robbing them of their dignity. Many of those serving prison sentences committed their crimes while under the influence of alcohol.

Among native youth, especially those who are poor, consumption of volatile solvents, inhalants, and even gasoline causes damage to their ability to function mentally and/or physically.

There have been a number of speculations about the patterns and causes of substance abuse in the Canadian indigenous population, including social pressure, coping strategies, cultural loss, defiance and boredom. A WHO report (1996, p. 39) suggests that in the 1990s alcohol, narcotics and hallucinogens were the most widely abused substances among the Canadian indigenous population. Alcohol is the most heavily consumed substance among urban aboriginal people. In recent years the use of inhalants and gasoline among children and youth has become a serious concern with tragic consequences.

The Nechi Institute (in Canada) is a successful indigenous-owned and staffed programme which relies on cultural values and spirituality with special emphasis on the re-introduction and practice of traditional ceremonies, which are considered by indigenous peoples to be essential for community wellness and empowerment (ibid. p. 40).

In preventive programmes for indigenous people, it is critical to understand their cultural values and their vision of life and the universe. To overcome the dilemma of alcohol and other substances of abuse, the following features of community life of indigenous peoples are important:

Resilience: Indigenous peoples possess inherent qualities of resilience and strength through their traditions, which enable them to endure hardship. Close bonding and social networking within the community reinforce this resilience. In spite of this, alcohol and drug abuse have been very destructive.

Cultural revitalization: Cultural activities and revitalization create bonds and strengthen the healing process.

Elders: Elders possess experience and knowledge and are highly respected in the community. They can help to empower those in trouble. In Canada, elders visit youth incarcerated in institutions, conduct ceremonies, and act as advisors and confidants at treatment centres.

Role of women: In the indigenous population worldwide, women tend to drink less than men and form the majority of abstainees. Women are often a valuable source of community strength and have to bear the brunt of alcohol or other drug abuse related to family violence while striving to nurture and care for children. Although women have been involved in the production of alcohol in some countries, in others, such as Australia, women have formed a strong anti-alcohol group, and in Micronesia they have contributed to strict legislation to control the availability of alcohol (ibid. pp. 84–5).

3

DRUG ABUSE IN CHILDREN AND YOUTH

Parents are not only role models but also providers of a healthy or polluted environment. They will influence their children's behaviour vis-à-vis the more available substances such as alcohol, marijuana and cigarettes. These factors, together with peer pressure, have been subjects of research studies.

A recent Canadian study of childhood predictors of smoking in adolescence is very intriguing. Margaret Becklake and colleagues (2005, p. 377) reported that in their follow-up study of Montreal schoolchildren, they found that children who were exposed to second-hand smoke during their childhood were more likely to become active smokers after puberty when they entered high school. These researchers found that salivary cotinine (a measure of uptake of environmental tobacco smoke) during the childhood of the study group was a significant predictor of adolescent smoking habits. It is possible that efficient absorption of nicotine from second-hand tobacco smoke during their childhood contributed to their susceptibility to nicotine-seeking behaviour. The high-school environment and peer pressure during puberty probably enhanced this development.

This finding, although needing further exploration, will have implications for anti-smoking intervention programmes, which could be also directed at susceptible individuals such as the children of smokers. A similar principle applies to the children of alcoholic parents or those who inhale marijuana, although the mechanism may be different.

Street children and drugs

In 1997 UNICEF estimated that there were about 100 million street children worldwide. By region it was estimated that there were 40 million in Latin America, 25–30 million in Asia and over 10 million in Africa. Although most of these children had a family or somewhere to sleep at night, an estimated five per cent of them were completely abandoned. Street children were mostly boys (71–97 per cent), but girls tended to suffer worse consequences because of sexual exploitation and transmission of diseases such as HIV/AIDS ('Drugs and young people', in UN 1997, p. 83). Street children are usually younger in developing countries than in developed countries.

Although the phenomenon of street children is not something new, recent economic and political changes, civil unrest, increasing family disintegration and natural disasters have led to larger numbers of children migrating from rural towns to the streets of larger cities. Some street children are born on the streets to older street children, some come from families who can no longer support them due to poverty, some are members of families who live on the streets, and others come to the streets after being orphaned. WHO (1993) estimated that there will be 16 million children orphaned by AIDS in Africa by 2015.

Living on the streets and its associated lifestyle make street children vulnerable to a range of health and other problems which are not typically experienced by other young people. Factors associated with the aetiology of their street existence include: family breakdown; armed conflict; poverty; natural and man-made disasters; famine; physical and sexual abuse; exploitation by adults; dislocation through migration; urbanization and overcrowding; and acculturation. Factors associated with the physical conditions of street life include: poor hygiene and sanitation; poor diet; lack of shelter; violence; transience of situation and its effects on planning; possible lack of positive attachments with consequent emotional, social, and sensory deprivations.

While street children may use drugs to keep awake for work or alert to possible violence, to get to sleep, to anaesthetize physical or emotional pain, or to replace the need for food, such drugs increase health risks and may lead to exploitation and violence.

Street children usually use drugs that are cheap and available, such as solvents in industrial areas, coca paste and cocaine in coca-producing areas, opium and opiates in opium-producing regions, and various forms of inhalants, alcohol, nicotine, cannabis and pharmaceutical products. In developing countries, street children don't fit the stereotype of the 'addict' or 'junkie' which exists in more developed nations – and who is often someone who may be anti-social or criminal, makes use of multiple drugs and injects heroin or other drugs. Rather, street children who use drugs in developing countries are friendly, cheerful, generous, resourceful, and helpful to each other.

Particularly prevalent among children and youth is the inhalation of solvents and commercial aerosols, an activity that has increased rapidly over the past decade. Inhalant abuse or 'glue sniffing' is attractive to children and adolescents because of easy access, low cost and powerful effect. The abuse of solvents by street children has become widespread in Latin America, Africa and Central and Eastern Europe, as well as in industrialized countries such as Australia, Canada and the United States. In Brazil and Mexico, solvents rank second after cannabis as the preferred substance of abuse among children: 5–10 per cent of the children in those countries abuse solvents.

Cities in the developing world are fast becoming overcrowded areas of destitute children trapped in a circle of poverty and drug addiction. India is thought to have the largest number of street children in the world: Bombay, Calcutta and New Delhi each have an estimated 100,000 street children. A growing number are involved in crime, with the juvenile delinquency rate of 3.1 per 1,000. The illicit drug industry can be seen by street children as offering a means of economic survival and a source of peer respectability. Drugs themselves offer a convenient, if temporary escape from reality (PEDDRO 1998).

Youth and drugs in society

During recent years there has been a worldwide increase in the use of illicit drugs among youth and young adults as they face more and more life stress and anxiety (UN 1997, p. 54). Most research into drug use prevalence suggests that illicit consumption declines from the late 20s and that few individuals initiate drug use after the age of 29.

Most studies suggest that there is a correlation between age of initiation of drug use and drug dependence (ibid. p. 83). Earlier onset in the consumption of drugs is associated with a more intense and wider use of other drugs at a later time (ibid. p. 51) and with more severe and long-term consequences for health, education and emotional development (ibid. p. 83). A study examining the way in which young people begin to inject drugs reported that the average age of the first injection was 16.2 years and that the most common drugs being injected were amphetamines (77 per cent). Of this 77 per cent, 88 per cent had used them before by means other than injection. In addition, 82.5 per cent of the subjects reported having been under the influence of some drug at the time of their injection (ibid. p. 66).

The World Bank states that on average drug users fall within the age group of 15–44, although most are in their mid-twenties (World Bank 1993, p. 89). In Latin America, however, the age group is younger, 12–22 years. Drug use is more likely to occur in families where there is a lack of meaningful communication and parental affection, or in families which approve and model drug use. Violence in the home seems to be one of the most important factors predisposing adolescents to initiate drug use (UN 1997, p. 78). 'A Brazilian survey of drug use among high school students reported that the incidence of drug use was more than 5 times greater among adolescents living with domestic violence compared to adolescents living without violence' (ibid. p. 52).

Illicit drug use in adolescents is often associated with other 'risk-taking' behaviours such as alcohol abuse, sexual involvements and higher than average levels of delinquent behaviours (ibid. p. 83). Sensation-seeking traits (impulsiveness, thrill-seeking) and a

The Queen of Sweden speaks out on drug use by young people

On 8 June 1998 Her Majesty the Queen of Sweden spoke at a conference sponsored by the United Nations in New York. This conference was held on the occasion of the UN's Special Session of the General Assembly on the world drug problem. In her keynote address to the panel on children, young people and drug abuse she made the following remarks:

> ... I have come here today not only as the Queen of my country, but, and more importantly, as a mother of three and as someone who cares very much about the problems facing young people today. One of the gravest problems we have to face together, among many, is that of drug abuse. For me, part of this is to take a public stance to support a society free of drug abuse.
>
> Young people use drugs for many different reasons. Some just want to copy their peers, to be 'cool'. Is this a valid reason? It can never be 'cool' to be out of control.
>
> Others have much more compelling reasons: to alleviate hunger, to forget their miseries, to block out fear, to tackle the crisis of a changing body during adolescence, to get away from sexual and physical abuse. In some instances you may find yourself in situations where you see no other way out. I believe there are many other, and more positive and beneficial ways to respond to such problems. That is why I have come here today ...
>
> ...What can be started can also be stopped ...
>
> ... Illicit drugs have never been more easily available than today, despite the massive efforts by governments to limit their supply. This is why I believe, that if we are to reach a stage where drug abuse no longer constitutes a problem, we must make sure that the demand is drastically reduced. And this you can only do by offering positive alternatives to drug abuse and by helping people deal with and refuse the offer of drugs and by helping to fill the void ...

... Those who have tried, discover that despite any short-term rush of satisfaction, drugs do not offer a long-term solution to needs or problems. They may hide some symptoms, but the underlying causes will still be there. Some people claim that drug use is a question of freedom of choice. Intoxication offers a chance to escape. But, it also means that the struggle for the good things in life, for one's own well-being and for the positive development of the children and the family, becomes a secondary issue. Instead of confronting the problems of every-day life, one chooses to run away – and drugs offer an escape route. For me this is not freedom. No! Quite the contrary . . .

... I think that the fact that an increasing number of chil-dren and young people use drugs is a message to us as adults and as parents. Young people from different countries of the world tell us that using drugs is an expression of the fact that they do not feel part of the society in which they live.

Source: Renate Bernadotte née Sommerlath. Talk given on the occasion of the General Assembly Special Session on the World Drug Problem, United Nations, 8 June 1998.

demand for immediate gratification may contribute to initial drug use (ibid. p. 57). The results of a study by Jessor and Jessor (cited ibid. p. 50) suggest that adolescents who are the most susceptible to illicit drug taking are those who 'are concerned with autonomy, have a lack of interest in the goals of conventional society, have a jaundiced view of society, have a more tolerant view of deviance, perceive less parental support and less compatibility between friends and paren-tal expectations, are more influenced by friends than by parents and have more support from friends for the drug taking behaviour.' It seems that the quality of the adolescents' relationship with their parents (especially the mother) is one of the most important pro-tective factors against the use of drugs (ibid. p. 59).

Some reasons given by adolescents for experimenting with illicit drugs are: to cope with stress, depression, anxiety and isolation, and living in a chaotic world. Other reasons include: curiosity, 'my friends were doing it' and 'there didn't seem to be any reason not to' (ibid. p. 49). Thus, another factor contributing to the consumption of illicit drugs by adolescents is the 'normalization' of drug use. Normalization of drug use refers to the extent to which a particular drug use may be considered 'normal' in a society, in that it is widespread, visible and fairly resistant to law-enforcement interventions (ibid. p. 48). The growing popularity of the amphetamine-type stimulants such as ecstasy provides an example of the normalization of drug use. Young ravers perceive oral ingestion of ecstasy (it is rarely injected) as 'normal', fashionable, safe and clean (ibid. p. 85). However, in condoning this behaviour as 'normal', society is distorting the concept of normality, conferring it on a practice which in reality is extremely unhealthy and harmful.

Although adolescence can be a time of experimentation with licit and illicit substances, most young people who experiment with drugs do not become dependent on them and they eventually stop. Bonding is important and may occur within three distinct groups: the family, the school, and the peer group. Young people who have developed strong positive attachments to their family and/or schoolwork are less likely to establish attachments to drug user peer groups. Young people who are detached from their families are at greatest risk of using drugs (WHO 1993).

Adolescence is an important time for developing coping strategies and skills. This process is dependent on having positive attachments, the opportunity to learn skills and an absence of overwhelming stressors. If a young person has the chance to develop effective coping skills, when a stressful situation occurs he or she will be less likely to choose to use drugs as a coping strategy. These skills may be cognitive or behavioural. Cognitive skills include skills such as self-assurance and self-control. Behavioural skills include problem-solving, assertiveness, communication skills, social networking, engaging in alternative activities and relaxation (ibid.).

Children, youth and alcohol

Under-age drinking is influenced by a number of factors including parental attitude, peers and the media. The advertising of drinking has been acknowledged by teenagers as an important influence. Popular magazines with high youth readership in particular have been influenced by alcohol companies to advertise alcoholic beverages. The average age at which young people (ages 12–17) begin to drink is 13 years old (*Globe* 2004b, p. 11). The age gap between boys and girls in drinking has been narrowing and has now almost disappeared. Children who begin drinking regularly by the age of 13 are more than four times as likely to become alcoholics as those who delay alcohol use until they are 21 years or older (*Globe* 1998, p. 8).

The consumption of alcohol as a 'drug of choice' has been on the rise in the United States and Europe. According to the National Research Council/Institute of Medicine (*Globe* 2004a), alcohol is the most frequently used drug among America's youth (more frequent than the use of tobacco or marijuana). Each day, more than 7,000 kids under the age of 16 take their first drink. The following observations were noted (ibid. p. 10):

- 1 in 5 eighth-graders is a current drinker.
- 1 in 5 youth aged 12–20 binge drinks (5 or more drinks on one occasion).
- Most kids drink to get drunk: more than 90 per cent of the alcohol consumed by 12–20-year-olds is taken when they are bingeing.
- Each day, three teenagers in the United States die from drinking and driving and at least six more die from other alcohol-related causes.
- Teenage girls who binge drink are up to 63 per cent more likely to become teenage mothers.
- Under-age drinking costs the United States $53 billion a year in medical care, lost productivity, and the pain and suffering of young drinkers.

Drugs and their defenceless victims

Individuals may accept or reject medical knowledge about the effects of drugs and alcohol, depending on their values and their way of life. They judge for themselves and take the consequences. But who will speak for those who have no voice in this world, have no authority over the decisions made for them and who are totally dependent on the lifestyle and habits of those who bear them? Such are the unborn children, the defenceless victims of parents who are alcohol or drug addicts. They have no conscious knowledge or awareness of what they might be exposed to at present or suffer from in the future, nor could they protest even if they were aware of undesirable drug effects. This is that segment of society which is not included in statistics, but is classified as disadvantaged even before being born.

1. *Effects on the unborn child.* It has been reported (Herrington 1980, p. 3) that

> nearly 50% of babies of heroin addicts are born too small, usually premature, compared with about 10% of the general population. This low birth weight carries with it a death risk 40 times that of normal weight infants, as well as an increased incidence of cerebral palsy, mental deficiency, terminal malformation, emotional disturbance, and visual and hearing defects. They are also more at risk from respiratory distress syndrome, (including newborn asphyxia), hypoglycemia, anaemia, infection, and other problems.

In 1980 it was estimated that about 126,000 women of childbearing age were heroin users in the United States, and this figure did not include those who were addicted to other abused substances (ibid.). According to the National Institute on Drug Abuse, in 1977 there were at least 4,742 infants known to have been born to addicted mothers in the United States (ibid.). This shows the extent of the 'pollution of the womb' of mothers in one of the most industrialized and progressive nations in the world. Although the passage of any substance through the placenta depends on a number of elements, including the placental blood flow and its metabolism of drugs, the molecular weight of the substances in question is important. Compounds with a molecular weight of less than 600 can pass through the placenta and reach the unborn child (Ling and Boutle 1979, p. 10). Many abused substances, such as alcohol, narcotics, barbiturates and tranquillizers, appear to be able to pass through the placenta and pose a threat to the health of the foetus.

Exposure to cannabis during pregnancy is known to have toxic effects on the foetus. Experiments on animals show that the placenta accumulates THC (cannabis extract) to a greater degree than the foetal tissues. However, the placenta's release of this substance into the foetus is slow. Thus the placenta serves both as a potential barrier against, and a reservoir for, the transfer of THC to the foetus (Alcoholism and Drug Addiction Research Foundation 1981). Cannabis-related substances can also be secreted into the milk of the nursing mother. Moreover, they can impair lactation as a result of THC's central effect on the brain and its probable reduction of the prolactin hormone. Consequently, neonatal malnourishment may occur, leading to a delay in weight gain and skeletal growth and an increase in the risk of neonatal mortality (ibid.). Whether other developmental impediments will appear in later years is not clearly known at present.

George Ling, Director of the Division of Narcotic Drugs at the United Nations' Vienna International Centre, wrote, 'to be born addicted to narcotics is surely one of the cruellest ways to enter the world; yet such is the fate of an increasing number of infants born to heroin-dependent mothers' (Ling and Boutle, p. 10).

One of the most remarkable research developments in the 1970s was the discovery of the effect of alcohol on pregnancy. It was during this period that researchers identified the presence of 'foetal alcohol syndrome' among mothers with chronic alcoholism. This syndrome is reported to affect from 1 in 300 to 1 in 2,000 infants and is characterized by pre-natal and post-natal growth retardation, neurological abnormalities including mental retardation, poor coordination, and hyperactivity. Research findings also indicate other abnormalities including microcephaly and defects in the eyes, ears, mouth and in the muscular, skeletal and cardiac systems (Sokol 1981). Moreover, as a result of heavy alcohol consumption during pregnancy, the following adverse effects have been reported: high incidence of spontaneous abortion (miscarriage), congenital anomalies, low birth weight, intra-uterine growth retardation, neonatal depression and other abnormalities (ibid.).

In the United States it has been estimated that the proportion of women who drink heavily during pregnancy ranges from 2 per cent to 13 per cent (ibid.). It appears that the risk of giving birth to a child with foetal alcohol syndrome is greater among women in a more advanced alcoholic condition. All these present a challenge to society at large and to the childbearing woman in particular for the responsibility that she faces in consuming alcohol while pregnant. There are also some indications that alcoholic fathers play a role in the development of foetal abnormalities; however, research in this area is still in progress. The exact mechanism of the effect of alcohol in the father on the sperm or through genetic transmission is not yet clear. But children of alcoholic parents are known to be more at risk for the development of congenital abnormalities.

2. *Effects on the breast-fed child.* Nature provides young infants with a healthy, pure and ideal nutrition: the breast milk of the mother. This ideal nutrition, however, is not immune from the effect of alcohol or drugs consumed by mothers. The extent of chemical contamination depends both on the quantity of drugs consumed and their cumulative effects. There is, for example, evidence to suggest that ingestion of alcohol to excess may affect breast milk and consequently produce drunkenness in the baby (Ananth 1978).

Although medical knowledge at present does not find moderate drinking by the mother harmful for the breast-fed infant, medical technology is not sufficiently advanced to produce sensitive tests which can accurately measure the reaction of the brain cells of a growing baby to the alcohol in his mother's milk. What should be borne in mind is that there are indications to suggest that ethanol reaches the breast milk in a concentration similar to that found in the peripheral blood (ibid.).

Morphine and heroin are also excreted through breast milk. Nursing mothers who are addicted to these substances and make regular use of them will foster a drug dependency in their infants. Medical experience shows that in the nursing mother addicted to heroin, sudden withdrawal of the drug is followed by symptoms of drug withdrawal not only in the mother, but also in the breast-fed baby. In such circumstances, re-administration of the drug to the addicted mother improved the withdrawal symptoms of the baby (ibid.). Babies of pregnant women who are addicted to narcotics such as morphine and heroin face the threat of critical withdrawal symptoms after birth when the narcotic, transmitted to them through the placenta, is no longer available. Unless the physician in charge is aware of this predicament and is prepared for thera-peutic intervention, the outcome may be serious. Depending on the extent of drug dependence in the mother, withdrawal symptoms in the baby may be mild and transient, or severe and life-threatening. In the nursing mother with a narcotic addiction, weaning the infant must be gradual to avoid a drug withdrawal reaction.

4

IMPACT OF PARENTAL ALCOHOLISM
ON CHILDREN AND YOUTH[*]

The family is the foundation and wellspring of human society. It
is a miniature of the nation; changes in the family are reflected
in society. The family as a system is influenced by environmental, biological, psychosocial and spiritual parameters. It evolves
according to socio-cultural norms and values. To understand the
impact of parental alcoholism on children and family we need to
examine the nature and development of family life and the needs
of individual members of the family. Alcohol and drug abuse is
not merely a medical issue; it reflects a psychological and spiritual crisis within a person. Each family creates its own culture
and pattern of behaviour. Home provides the first family environment in which a child begins to learn about life. Parents are seen
as behavioural models to follow. Attitudes and concepts towards
the consumption of alcohol as something acceptable and healthy,
or completely the opposite, are formed during this period.

The breaking of family bonds and the disruption of parental
relationships have rendered these vital units of human society
more vulnerable to the disturbing forces of drugs and alcohol.

---

[*] The original version of this chapter was presented by A-M.
    Ghadirian and N. Ghadirian at the World Forum on Substance
    Abuse, September 2002, Montreal, Canada.

Family and Alcoholism

In a Canadian study, it was found that adolescents living in single-parent or mixed marriages (marriage in which one parent is not the biological parent) showed higher risk of dangerous behaviour. 'Compared with children living with both natural parents, these children were seven times more likely to smoke cigarettes, five times more likely to use cannabis and eight times more likely to use other drugs, four times more likely to exhibit delinquent behaviour and three times more likely to drink heavily' (European Commission 1998, p. 16).

It has been reported (ibid. p. 17) that in England, children who experienced parental divorce during their childhood were later involved in heavy or problem drinking. Even among divorcees of all ages and both sexes, there was a greater risk of illness and mortality as compared with married couples.

According to the European Commission report, problematic drinking can disrupt the division of labour and responsibility within the family framework. When a family member, e.g. father, becomes alcoholic, he may cease to perform as a breadwinner. Consequently, his function is performed by the spouse or another member of the family or, at times, by no one.

Alcohol problems can also upset the family's social life. Special events such as birthdays or anniversaries may not be celebrated because of a fear of disruption by the alcoholic parent. In such an environment, family life becomes unpredictable, fraught with fear and embarrassment. Marital conflicts as well as domestic violence and abuse occur frequently in this kind of dysfunctional family. In fact, an alcohol problem in the family can be a significant predictor of violence in the family (ibid. p. 21).

Parental impact of alcoholism

Alcohol and other substances of abuse interfere with the availability and quality of care and responsibility of parents, especially mothers, for their children. Alcoholism can adversely affect maternal bonding and child development. Children of parents with alcoholism are more prone to accidents and behavioural disorders. Family violence and antisocial behaviour are more likely to erupt in these families. The family's relationship with alcohol is a two-way affair: while the consumption of alcohol will impact on family life, family conflict itself can lead to drinking problems (Figure 2).

Figure 2
A two-way affair

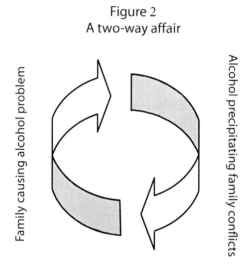

There are indications that children of alcoholic parents are at greater risk of emotional, sexual and other physical abuses. Marital breakdown as a result of parental drinking and abuse are not uncommon. The mental health of children of alcoholics is often neglected. Wife-battering and other forms of abuse of the spouse may often go unreported because of the fear of reprisal, rejection or family breakdown. The impact of alcohol on the foetus (foetal alcohol syndrome) is well established and these children show psychological and biological changes in their development.

Genetic vulnerability

In the biological aspects of alcoholism, genetic transmission plays an important role. Results of genetic studies show that although genetic factors contribute to the development of alcoholism, there is a considerable variability in this genetic transmission; some of the children of alcoholics may not develop alcoholism. Other factors, therefore, such as psychosocial and environmental elements may influence the predisposition of children to alcoholism. It is not the alcoholism itself which is inherited by the children of alcoholics, rather it is the underlying vulnerability to alcoholism which is genetically transmitted. In families where one parent is alcoholic, in order for a child to become alcoholic there is a need for precipitating factors to kindle the vulnerability. This kindling effect may be due to a number of factors such as marital conflict, violence in the family, parental loss, separation or divorce, easy availability of alcohol, and a history of drug abuse in the family.

Alcohol and pregnancy

In pregnant women, alcohol crosses the placenta and reaches the unborn infant. After birth, alcohol enters the mother's breast milk and is consumed by the child who is highly vulnerable at this tender age. It has been estimated that for pregnant women who consume three drinks of alcohol a day there is a 10 per cent chance of giving birth to a baby with foetal alcohol syndrome (FAS). This rate rises to 33 per cent if the mother consumes six drinks per day (DuPont 1984, p. 111). Children born to alcoholic women are not only at risk for lower weight, but also for cardiac defects, neurological impairments, and learning deficits. Foetal alcohol syndrome is characterized by growth deficiency, poor motor development, irritability and mental retardation which may begin before birth and develop throughout childhood (ibid.). These children may also show symptoms of hyperactivity.

Dysfunctional alcoholic families bring about dysfunctional children. For example, sons of alcoholics are four times more at risk for developing alcoholism than those in the general population. In a study of 408 adult children of alcoholics matched with normal controls, Mathew et al. (1993) reported the following findings. Male children of alcoholics showed higher rates of alcohol and drug abuse and greater antisocial symptoms than did the female children of alcoholics. Male children of alcoholics also had a significantly higher rate of lifetime diagnoses of alcohol and drug abuse than men who were not children of alcoholics. On the other hand, more female children of alcoholics showed generalized anxiety disorder as compared with girls or women who were not children of alcoholics.

Sons of alcoholic fathers had a higher prevalence of substance abuse and showed more antisocial behaviour than did daughters of alcoholic fathers. Daughters of alcoholic fathers, on the other hand, were noted to have a higher rate of generalized anxiety disorder. As compared with children of non-alcoholic parents, adult children of alcoholics had significantly higher prevalence rates of phobia, generalized anxiety disorder, panic disorder and agoraphobia (ibid.).

Alcohol is thus a major health and social concern in many countries of the world. Ten to fifteen per cent of Americans suffer from alcoholism and 28–34 million people are children of alcoholics (ibid.).

In our study of 206 high-school students in Montreal (Ghadirian et al. 1986), we found that 18.5 per cent of students had a member of the family who drank heavily. Fourteen per cent of students reported that their fathers were 'heavy drinkers' while 13 per cent noted that their mothers were using 'nerve pills'. There was a positive correlation between the 'heavy drinker' parents and their amphetamine user children (10%) in the total sample of amphetamine users.

Child Abuse and Neglect

Children of alcoholics are at greater risk of neglect and physical and sexual abuse by the affected parents. Reports on the extent and prevalence of child abuse vary depending on the history of recent alcohol abuse or long-term drinking (from 4% to 43%).

The rate is much higher among North American Indians (100%) (Zeitlin 1994).

Consumption of alcohol leads to the disinhibition of the individual. Children, being young and defenceless, are often easy prey for abusive alcoholic parents. Maternal drinking may impair not only the mother's daily functioning but also her role in protecting her children. In such a situation, father–daughter incest may become a reality. Many incest victims are women who are also alcoholic and who began drinking at an early age. But abuse of alcohol by itself does not constitute the specific cause of incest or other abuses; there are many other contributing factors to be taken into consideration such as parental personality disorder, socio-economic circumstances and cultural attitudes (ibid.).

Although parental alcoholism is often associated with family violence, separation or divorce, one should also keep in mind other parameters which may contribute to drinking by the parents in the first place, such as losses, job stress and unemployment, interpersonal conflicts, competitive lifestyle, emotional and character disorders, and so on.

Parental drinking creates a great deal of stress, fear and uncertainty in the children, who feel unprotected at home and unprepared for society to cope with external stressors. As a result of loss of basic trust in the protecting capacity of the drinking parent, the children feel unsafe and insecure. Unless a healthy spouse of the alcoholic person effectively compensates for the failures of the alcoholic partner, a disorganization of family life and deterioration of parental care are most likely to occur. Children in such a family, however, sometimes out of necessity, may develop a new bonding among themselves to protect one another.

Children of alcoholics have a higher rate of trouble with the law, history of antisocial behaviour (especially among males) and greater incidence of depression, (especially among females). There is a high incidence of anxiety and hyperactivity disorders. Their self-esteem is low and they are more susceptible to drinking (ibid.).

47

What children say about alcoholic parents

In a report prepared by the European Commission (1998), the following statements by children of families where one or both parents were alcoholic were reported.

- 'Dad gets drunk every day, he hits me and mum . . . He broke my arm once. If I have bruises he . . . stops me going to school. He says if we ever tell anyone he will kill us . . . I'm scared . . . it's getting worse. *(Girl)*
- 'Dad drinks and hits mum, I took an overdose last week, I want to die. I can't talk to mum, it would only add to her problems . . . It's all my fault. *(Girl)*
- 'Please don't stop my mother smoking . . . I would rather she smoked than drank.' *(Boy with foetal alcohol syndrome)*
- 'Sometimes it's hard. I can't run away because when there's trouble there will be no one to run to for help.' *(Boy)*
- 'I cry . . . she (the mother) says she will quit, but it never happens.' *(Girl)*
- 'If other parents knew about my father drinking, they might stop their children playing with me.' *(Boy)*
- 'Mum says Dad is drinking again. Dad says he isn't . . . I am confused. I'll just try harder to work it out.' *(Tasha, 7)*

(European Commission, 1998, p. 6)

What parents say about their own or others' alcohol problem

In the same report (p. 7), the following statements were reported:

- 'I felt responsible for everything. I was constantly blaming myself for having chosen this partner and the consequent effect it had on my children.' (*Wife*)
- 'He is prepared to lose his family rather than stop drinking. He mustn't love us and I find myself wondering if he ever did or if all our life together was a lie. I feel sad and frightened and angry.' (*Wife*)
- 'I felt let down and I could not cope. I felt she had given up on

all the plans we had made when we got married – given up on the kids and everything.' (*Husband*)

On problem drinking:

- 'I made myself believe I was a good father taking my son to football. Now I admit I did it to have an excuse to have some beers . . . He (the son) has more than once found me on the floor drunk and in coma. I do not know what it means to a child to see his father like that.' (*Father, now abstinent*)
- 'The caller said he saw the two-year-old wandering down the road wearing a T-shirt, underpants and socks. The caller asked him where he lived and the child took him to a house 200–300 yards away. The front door was open and a man and a woman were asleep on a sofa in a cigarette-smoke-filled room which also smelled of alcohol. The child went to the woman, calling her "Mummy" and shook her. She told him to "bugger off".' (*Neighbour*)
- 'My strongest childhood memory is one of fear. My father was a huge man and always angry . . . He would sit up drinking late at night. My brother, sister and I were terrified of being beaten . . .' (*Tim, 53*)

Interestingly, while parental alcoholic behaviour may be associated with child sexual abuse, it also appears that, especially among women, childhood sexual abuse is associated with problem drinking later in life. However, it is to be noted that not all children of alcoholic parents develop behavioural problems.

Alcoholism and Family Dynamics

The family is not only a sacred institution, it is also like a workshop for learning and life experiences. A healthy family is characterized by a dynamic, interactive, nurturing and loving environment which encourages learning skills to cope with life and its challenges.

Addictions of any kind, especially alcoholism, adversely affect the stability and developmental process in family life. It is important to explore and understand the dynamics of interpersonal relation-ships in the family of the addict. Guilt and dependency play an important role in the dynamics of family relationships.

In terms of character, it has been noted that in a family with addiction problems mothers tend to be indulgent, overprotective and permissive (D'Agnone and Basyk 1989) while fathers have one of two opposing features: either ineffectual, distant or absent; or violent and with authoritarian attitudes. The son is often treated as a favourite, a child easy to handle (ibid.).

The equilibrium of the family relationship often revolves around the addict. For example, if a child or teenager is an addict, parents may strive for greater cohesion and direct their efforts toward that child, setting aside their own personal conflicts. When the child improves, however, parents may resume their conflicts and even split up. Alternatively, one of the parents may get depressed and the other show psychosomatic symptoms. Likewise, the siblings may act out emotionally. Such a disequilibrium in the family rela-tionship may cause the problem child to feel guilty. This child may consequently resume taking drugs to restore family equilibrium and the cycle may go on (ibid.). For the treatment of the addict member of the family, this family dynamic needs to be recognized, with the aim of bringing about harmony in the parent–child rela-tionship while avoiding substance abuse. If such a development succeeds, the family becomes a self-regulating therapeutic envi-ronment. In such a family there is greater parental involvement in the psychosocial development of children, with a higher degree of caring and sharing.

Besides socio-cultural forces, the economic conditions of fam-ilies may be linked to the drinking of the offspring. In one study, American families showed a positive correlation between high economic status and adolescent drinking behaviour. But when this finding was compared with that of the Japanese families, the trend was the reverse (Chassin and Barrera 1991).

In some families with alcoholic or drug-addicted parents, children may be forced into a precocious early adulthood role of caring and protecting younger siblings. They may even have to look after their addicted and dysfunctional parents. They are deprived of their basic rights of receiving proper parental care and education. To survive the pressure of poverty, these children may have to do menial labour or become involved in drug trafficking or prostitution in order to gain revenue for their disabled parents and themselves. Those who refuse such an oppressive environment at home may escape to the streets only to discover other forms of abuse and another violent world.

Prevention

Contrary to general assumptions, it is not only the addict who needs support; serious attention should be paid to the well-being and emotional needs of the entire family. The problem of alcoholism in a family member is not only an individual problem; it is a family problem. Society must be educated to understand the nature and consequences of parental alcoholism and to develop proper skills in coping with life stress. The family needs to become a healing environment where the alcoholic member is not alienated or removed, but rather cared for, communicated with and understood. Love and unity within the family can empower the family members to acknowledge and confront the problem together, with care and proper treatment. Preventive education is a multidimensional process that requires the acquisition of knowledge and insight into the nefarious consequences of alcoholism and the development of psychological and spiritual insights and abilities to prevent addictive behaviour.

5

GENDER AND SUBSTANCE ABUSE

Although males are known to surpass females in all forms of drug abuse, emerging information indicates alarming drug problems among females which have not appeared in official statistics. Women are often wives, siblings, mothers or daughters of drug-abusing males. Through their traditional role of nurturing and providing family support, females shield males from the consequences of their abuse. As a result, these women suffer stressful challenges and in their effort to cope may themselves be drawn into alcohol or drug abuse (UN 1997, p. 79). With such a dysfunctional family life it is a perpetual struggle to survive amidst violence and poverty. Such an unhealthy environment of intimidation and despair, combined with a strong need to obtain drugs (i.e. cocaine or heroine), may compel women to become drug couriers or resort to sexual abasement and prostitution.

Women and Substance Abuse

An increasing number of women have become involved in the consumption of drugs and in some countries the cultivation, production, and even trafficking of these substances. For example, women are the major harvesters of opium in Asia and coca leaves in South America (ibid. p. 82).

Women are less likely than men to use illicit drugs, but are more likely to misuse tranquillizers, sedatives and analgesics for medical and non-medical purposes (ibid. p. 81). Two-thirds of long-term users of tranquillizers are women, with one-third over 64 years of age (Mellinger et al. 1994). This trend is worldwide and appears to be growing. In Guatemala, women are five times more likely to take tranquillizers than men; in Brazil, psychotropic drugs are prescribed twice more often for women than for men (UN 1997, p. 81). In Jamaica 35 per cent of women take pain-killers while only 18 per cent of men do so (ibid. p. 82). A study by Gutteman reported that physicians in North America were 2.5 times more likely to prescribe psychoactive drugs to women over 60 years than to men of the same age (cited ibid. p. 81).

Women and risk factors

Factors such as socioeconomics, parental drug use, childhood experiences, the influence of friends and poor impulse control have been identified as risk factors for substance abuse (ibid. p. 52). However, some risk factors for substance abuse are different for men and women. Also, post-traumatic stress disorder (PTSD) is more common in female than in male patients with drug abuse problems. The co-occurrence of psychiatric disorders (especially depression), illicit drug use and eating disorders is relatively high among women (M. D. Stein et al. 1997). Further research studies show that childhood sexual abuse has been associated with drug abuse in women. (Hurley et al. 1991; Rohsenow et al. 1988). Some studies indicate that up to 70 per cent of women in drug abuse treatment report histories of physical and sexual abuse (NIDA 1993). Alcoholic women are twice as likely as non-alcoholic women to have been beaten or sexually assaulted as a child (Winfield et al. 1990).

In cross-sectional studies it has been documented that women with eating disorders, including anorexia nervosa and bulimia, have higher rates of alcohol and other substances of abuse than those reported in the general female population (Beary et al. 1986, Kassett et al. 1989).

There is increasing evidence that the effects of drug abuse and addiction do not always impact men and women in the same way.

Female drug addicts are usually initiated into use by males (UN 1997, p. 80; Anglin et al. 1987). However, data indicate that for many illicit drugs, women may proceed more quickly to drug dependence than men. This observation has been made for women opiate addicts, cocaine addicts and alcoholics (Kosten et al. 1986; Griffin et al. 1989; Anglin et al. 1987). The progression to serious complications after a shorter duration of heavy drug use also creates different health risks for women (Piazza et al. 1989). The combined use of alcohol with psychoactive drugs presents serious health hazards for women of all ages, as it does for men.

Women are at high risk for conditions related to drug abuse such as hepatitis, tuberculosis and sexually transmitted diseases (UN 1997, p. 94). Syphilis in particular has been associated with crack use (R.A. Stein et al. 1997). Some studies showed that breast cancer, osteoporosis and menstrual dysfunction are more prevalent among women with alcohol abuse. As women differ from men with regard to the proportion of muscle, fat and water in their bodies, females develop alcohol-related liver diseases more rapidly and are less tolerant toward alcohol consumption (NGO World Forum 1994, p. 10).

One of the most devastating consequences of drug use in women is the risk of HIV/AIDS. The association between drug injection and HIV transmission has become a major concern in many parts of the world. Women are more at risk of acquiring infections such as HIV through their own use of contaminated needles to inject drugs or through sexual contact with drug users harbouring such a disease. A report from a North American study showed that 61 per cent of a total of 9,071 women with HIV/AIDS were also injecting drugs and 22 per cent of these had sexual partners who also injected drugs. (ibid.). 'Up to 46% of women's AIDS cases have been directly attributed to drug injection . . .' (NIDA 1993). Seventy per cent of women with HIV/AIDS have a history of illicit drug use (M. D. Stein et al. 1997). Women are at increased risk of contracting HIV because of the greater transmissibility from male to female.

Risk factors in pregnancy

An aspect of drug abuse by women that is of special concern is the use of drugs during pregnancy. Estimates of the incidence of substance abuse in pregnancy range from 0.5 to 25 per cent depending on the mode of identification and intensity of drug screening (ibid.). Research indicates that pregnant drug users are at an increased risk of spontaneous abortion, miscarriage, ectopic pregnancy, stillbirth, and low weight gain. Their newborn may have low birth weight, smaller head size and congenital malformation (ibid.).

Alcohol easily crosses into the blood through the placenta and affects the developing baby in the womb, and even after birth through the mother's milk to the infant. As a result of neurological and behavioural harm sustained through a maternal drinking problem, there is a greater likelihood of foetal alcohol syndrome (see also above, Chapter 3).

Stigma in society

Women may even experience worse consequences than men as a result of their involvement with drugs. They may be at higher risk of developing alcohol-related problems, such as severe liver disease, at lower levels of consumption than men (ibid.). Further, drug-abusing women are more likely to be stigmatized than their male counterparts because their behaviour is viewed by society as 'double deviant', that is: deviant from social norms (drug-taking is not socially acceptable) and deviant from the traditional roles of women as wife, mother and family nurturer (UN 1997, p. 80). Women who consume drugs regularly tend to become increasingly isolated from non-users, especially when, by trading sex, women alienate themselves further from society. Crack/cocaine markets in the United States have been associated with high rates of sexual promiscuity and with transactions entailing sexual debasement and abuse (ibid. p. 82).

Gender and Treatment Opportunities

Compared to men, women entering treatment for drug abuse are more likely to be depressed, to have encountered more opposition to treatment from family and friends and to perceive higher personal psychosocial costs (Allen 1994). In addition, these women have to face a variety of other barriers in order to enter treatment (UN 1997, p. 80). For example, they are more likely to be poor and without insurance than their male counterparts (M.D. Stein et al. 1997). Moreover, drug-addicted mothers are more likely to be single, separated or divorced and often are lacking community support, shelter, and financial assistance. They may decide not to seek treatment out of fear that the medical authorities may remove their children because of their drug habit (UN 1997, p. 80).

Historically, women have been protected by their later onset of drug use: for example, the onset of alcohol intake for women is relatively later than for men, but a woman may seek treatment at an earlier age than her male counterpart (Schukit 1995). However, the gender gap in drug and alcohol abuse is closing. While significantly fewer adult women than men use alcohol, cigarettes or illicit drugs, adolescent boys and girls have very similar patterns of drug use. During adolescence, girls and boys are as likely to drink or use illicit drugs, with the age of first drug use essentially the same. A common explanation for the increase in drug consumption among women is the global social and cultural advancement of the role of women from the traditional one as mother and homemaker to that of economic provider, a price paid for emancipation and equality in a male-dominated world (UN 1997, pp. 79–80).

Women and Alcoholism

According to Schukit (1995), when a woman is involved with alcohol or other substance abuse, it is less likely to be tolerated by family members and friends than a man's involvement would be, especially in developing countries. As a result women may conceal the extent and gravity of their problem.

Women who develop alcohol dependence are more likely to

have an alcoholic spouse, more family disruption and a greater probability of receiving psychiatric medications. Because there are more alcoholic men than women (twice as many), the likelihood that some women may have an alcoholic spouse is also strong. In fact, experience shows that women who grew up in a family where the father was alcoholic are more likely to choose an alcoholic husband or partner. In some families, the drug-abusing men become 'absent males' and thus the burden of financial support falls on the shoulders of the women who are also expected to take care of the children and home, as well as act as breadwinners. In a family where the spouse is a drug user, the money necessary for education, clothing, food and shelter is diverted to drugs and the family begins to disintegrate. In single families with alcoholic mothers, depression and financial difficulties further complicate life and child care.

Keeping Manipur dry

Women can be a powerful force in stemming the tide of alcohol abuse. According to a 1992 report (Bedi, p. 1) in the northeast Indian state of Manipur:

> Any man caught drinking by women on their nightly temperance patrols is in for trouble. He is likely to find himself stripped, tied atop a donkey and paraded through the streets with a blackened face before being locked up for the night promising never to drink again. The next morning he is handed over to the police, finally cooperating with the awesome Nupi Lan or 'Women's War Association' volunteers who, after decades of militant agitation, were successful in driving the Manipur state government to declare alcohol prohibition (in April 1991).
>
> Illegal rice-liquor distillation has increased since then and so have Nupi Lan patrols across the Manipur valley where around 350,000 men or roughly 45% of the male population were estimated to have a drinking problem.
>
> The vigil by hundreds of Maira Paibis or torchbearers, named after the paraffin torches they carry, is organized on a rotation

system from sunset to midnight in towns across the valley where a majority of the state's 1.3 million people live.

Positioning themselves at street corners, they whistle up reinforcements within minutes if they confront drunk males. The men are forced to say where the still is located and it is destroyed. Then the donkey treatment begins.

'Anyone caught by the Paibis never wants a repeat experience and is usually "cured" of drinking' said a Manipur government official. Senior government officials enjoy no immunity from the patrols and even casual drinkers make sure they are hundreds of miles away in New Delhi or Calcutta before daring to drink.

Women as mothers are not only the first educators of children, but they are also role models in providing health care and preserving the well-being of their children and family. Consequently, they are often involved in primary care of the sick in the family and decide about the type of drugs for colds or pain available over the counter. In most parts of the world, primary school teachers or school nurses are women and they are also providers of knowledge on health and hygiene. As the NGO World Forum on Drug Abuse concluded in 1994 (pp. 12–16) women therefore play a vital role in the attitude of the new generation of human society toward drugs and personal health.

6

HIV/AIDS AND SUBSTANCE ABUSE

AIDS (Acquired Immunodeficiency Syndrome) has become an epidemic which affects millions of people around the world. AIDS can be transmitted not only through sexual relationship but also through the injection of drugs. Contaminated needles, syringes and other injection equipment play an important role in the transmission of HIV/AIDS infection to those who don't have the disease. To be HIV- (Human Immune Virus) positive means that a person has been exposed to HIV or is infected by it; however, the chronic infection may take up to 10 years (or at times longer) to eventually destroy the immune system, at which time AIDS occurs.

Drug Injection and HIV Transmission

It is estimated that there are 13 million injecting drug users (IDUs) worldwide; 78 per cent of them live in developing and transition countries and the majority are young (*Globe* 2006, pp. 19–20). Drug injecting practice has been identified in more than 100 countries of the world of which the majority reported HIV infection among IDUs. In some countries the pattern of HIV transmission was affected by the IDUs. In Thailand, where drug consumers used to smoke opium, a gradual transition was made from opium to heroin smoking and eventually to heroin injection (from the

1950s to the 1970s) (UNDCP 1997, p. 32). Within 9 months, from January to September 1988, the rates of HIV increased from 1 per cent to 32–43 per cent. Likewise the number of AIDS patients among IDUs in Thailand increased from seven in 1990 to 691 in 1994. This is a stark testimony to the fact that the practice of injecting heroin (and needle exchange) played a major role in that development (ibid.).

In a sample of countries representing 61 per cent of the world's population, it was estimated that there was an average of 3–4 million IDUs. If this rate (105 IDUs per 100,000 population) were to be extended to the total world population, the number of IDUs worldwide could range as high as 5.5 million people (Mann et al. 1992, p. 407). Those drugs that are injected most vary from country to country and even within the same country, based on sociocultural attitudes and the types of drugs available. Their physiological effects may influence the frequency and pattern of their use. Drugs such as cocaine – which has a shorter duration of action – may require more frequent daily injection than heroin. Nevertheless, the main drug injected worldwide is heroin, followed by cocaine and amphetamines (ibid. p. 410).

In the past, it was believed that HIV/AIDS could be transmitted by injection only through intravenous injection. But recent findings show that it can also be transmitted through subcutaneous and intramuscular injection, and so the terminology of 'injection drug user' (IDU) has been more appropriately adopted (ibid.).

The reason for the popularity of injecting drugs is that it assures that a greater quantity of the drug reaches the brain more quickly and therefore has a greater effect. Sharing needles and syringes among drug users is a major cause of HIV/AIDS transmission, although many of them may also transmit the virus through sexual relationship.

The injection form of drug abuse is the most dangerous form of drug consumption, as the effect is immediate and the consequences can be serious. In most research studies, injection drug users are considered to be sexually active. The disinhibiting effect of alcohol and drugs influences human judgement and risk-taking behaviour, diminishing precautions in sexual relationships;

this in turn further increases the chance of transmission of disease through sexual interaction (UN 1997, p. 91). The exchange of needles and syringes further compounds the transmission of infections such as hepatitis B and HIV/AIDS.

In its *World Drug Report* for 1997 the UN International Drug Programme reported that in the United States the largest number of transmissions occurred through the sexual activity of gay men, while in Europe most HIV transmission occurred through injecting drug use (p. 88). This pattern, however, may be changing. About 22 per cent of the world's HIV/AIDS population inject drugs (p. 89). The number of IDUs varies from country to country: for example, in England it is 6 per cent while in Thailand it is 80 per cent (p. 91). Women seem to form a higher proportion of 'new injectors' (individuals injecting drugs for six years or less) and this category of injectors among women varies geographically from 25 per cent in New York to 69 per cent in Glasgow (p. 94).

In a recent collaborative epidemiological study (European Collaborative Study 2006, p. 1419) of mother-to-child transmission (MTCT) of HIV, data from 5,967 HIV-infected pregnant women and their infants were analysed. Among these, 4,716 were from Western/Central Europe and the rest were from the Ukraine (East). The results showed a shift among pregnant women of western Europe from having acquired HIV through drug injection to acquiring it from heterosexual activity. In Ukraine injecting drug use has also decreased.

IDUs and risk-taking behaviour

Injecting drug users are engaged in more risk-taking behaviour both in terms of the nature and pattern of their injection and their sexual activities. In a study of 300 young drug injectors in Australia, the incidence of sharing injecting equipment (needle/syringe) was reported to be 44.5 per cent (UN 1997, p. 57). Among these, both male and female IDUs had multiple sexual partners; the average age was 18.7 years with 11 per cent still attending school. Among the female participants in this study, there was a 53 per cent incidence rate of pregnancy, with an average age during the pregnancy of 16.4 years (ibid. p. 67). This study reflects the complexity and seriousness of injecting drug use in a permissive environment of young population. One wonders about the psychological and biological impact of injecting drug use and sexual permissiveness, not only on the pregnancy, but on the babies born from these young mothers. Their ability to foster a proper nurturing and caring environment for their children, let alone to educate them in such an unhealthy social climate, is questionable.

Many cocaine IDUs have a highly disorganized lifestyle and inject cocaine frequently. The emotional feeling of 'high' after injection, sexual involvement, poor hygiene, poverty and living on the street are just some of the factors that contribute to the spread of HIV/AIDS among these IDUs. This pattern of behaviour, although varying from person to person, makes this group of individuals more at risk of transmitting HIV/AIDS or other infectious diseases such as hepatitis and tuberculosis to one another. David Kosub reported (1997) that many cocaine IDUs inject themselves with cocaine 20–30 times a day and this, together with the high rate of needle exchange, can have a significant effect in the spread of HIV infection (p. 1). In Canada, the 1990s witnessed individuals becoming infected with HIV at a younger age and the infection rate was on the rise among both intravenous drugs users and women in the wider society, many of whom acquired HIV from sexual partners who were also IDUs (p. 52).

The Impact of HIV/AIDS on Children

Children affected by HIV/AIDS have received less attention because often people assume that AIDS is a disease which kills adults. Moreover, as the HIV virus is generally transmitted sexually or through injecting drug use, people tend to think that AIDS is an adult problem. However, according to UNAIDS and WHO estimates, more than four million children under the age of 15 have been infected with HIV since the epidemic began over two decades ago. More than 90 per cent of them were infants born to HIV-positive mothers who were infected with the virus before or during birth or through breastfeeding (WHO 2006).

In children HIV infection often progresses rapidly to AIDS; as a result, most of the children who have been infected have developed AIDS and the majority of them have died (ibid). It is not precisely clear what percentage of the parents of these children contracted HIV/AIDS through injecting drugs and it is more difficult to know if during their teenage years these children were involved in sexual or drug abuse activities with those infected with the HIV virus. Among the millions of street children around the globe are many who have been involved in drug abuse, trafficking or prostitution, which would make them vulnerable to HIV/AIDS at a young age.

The issue of decriminalization

The subject of the decriminalization of cocaine has been debated among experts and in society. But decriminalization does not appear to be a viable solution to the problem of infected needles; indeed, it may exacerbate it. For example, laboratory studies on rats show that when they are given unlimited access to injectable cocaine, the rats continue to self-administer cocaine until they collapse and die. The pleasure centre of the brain at the receiving end of cocaine seems to perpetuate the need to receive it repetitively. The frequency of drug injections depends not only on the character of the user, but also on the nature of the drug. For example, in IDUs who switch from heroin to cocaine there is a rise in the frequency of drug injection and needle exchange.

7

BIOLOGICAL FACTORS IN ADDICTION

No single factor has been identified as the cause of drug addiction; rather, there are a number of psychosocial and biological factors that contribute to drug abuse and the addiction process.

Endorphins as the Brain's Endogenous Opiates

Research studies show that the human brain releases substances that are similar to some psychoactive drugs. In the 1970s, as researchers were studying the effect of heroin on the brain, they discovered brain receptors with a specific affinity for morphine. This led them to search for natural neurotransmitters that would connect with the synapses of pleasure centres of the brain. The result was the discovery of peptides or chains of protein-building blocks called endogenous opioid peptides or endorphins. Some of the endorphins are the brain's own morphine-like substances (DuPont 1997, pp. 106–7). Endorphin, a neurotransmitter produced internally (inside the body) is part of the endogenous opiate system, as compared to morphine which is part of the exogenous opiate system (UNODC 1997, p. 46). Following this discovery it was speculated that there might be a relationship between drug dependency and genetic predisposition and that, as a result of some biological weaknesses in endogenous opiates, a person might seek out exogenous opiates, stimulants and other drugs to compensate.

However, a person may also develop drug dependency without any physical or biological deficiency as a result of peer pressure, stress or other psychosocial factors (see Chapter 8).

The Biology of Pleasure-seeking Behaviour

Many studies have been carried out on the pleasure and pain centres located in the midbrain, in order to unravel the mechanism of addiction. Laboratory animal experiments have demonstrated that repetitive electrical stimulation of pleasure centres of the brain sets a pattern of pleasure-seeking behaviour. Researchers found that rats with electrodes in their brains would work hard to experience electric stimulation of their pleasure centres (positive reinforcement). When stimulation of their closely related pain centres caused pain (negative reinforcement), they worked just as hard to avoid pain. 'The rats hooked up to the electrical stimulation pressed the bars to get pleasurable shocks to the point of exhaustion in preference to water, food, or even sex' (DuPont 1997, p. 111). When the same experiments were repeated on human beings, electrical stimulation of their pleasure centres induced not only a good feeling, but also a sense of euphoria and lower sensitivity to pain.

Robert DuPont, who has made significant contributions in the field of substance abuse and addiction, has pointed out in clinical observations that those addicted to alcohol or other drugs acted as if they were 'enslaved to immediate pleasure, despite the prospect of even catastrophic long-term negative consequences of their drug use' (ibid.). This viewpoint may challenge Sigmund Freud's notion that human psychical activity is bound to produce pleasure and avoid pain. The pleasure and pain centres are governed by neurotransmitters (the brain's messengers) that influence our behaviour. Substance abuse affects the pleasure centres in various ways and also inhibits the pain centres of the brain. It is the stimulating effects of drugs on pleasure centres and the reciprocal inhibition of pain and distress that motivates addicts to persist in their pleasure-seeking behaviour (ibid. p. 112).

The brain's pathways to addiction

The mesolimbic system of the brain plays an important role in addiction. Illicit substances activate the mesolimbic dopamine system which potentiates natural as well as pharmacological rewards. Drugs including opiates, stimulants, alcohol, nicotine and cannabis all act on the above system to increase the synaptic levels of dopamine. For natural rewards such as food and sex, dopamine is also released, but not in a sustained fashion (Self, p. 223).

Neurotransmitters: The brain's messengers

There are at least three major neurotransmitters that play an important role in the development of substance abuse and addiction. Dopamine (DA) is involved in the pleasure process, endorphin in pain and stress, and norepinephrine (NE) in fear and anger responses. DuPont (1997, p. 118) elaborated on the paths to the brain's pleasure centres as follows:

> All substances and behaviours that produce pleasure stimulate the brain's pleasure centers, the ventral tegmental area and the nucleus accumbens. Each pathway to the brain's pleasure centers is unique, but all can produce addiction in people who are vulnerable. The major protections from addiction are lack of availability and cultural warnings about prohibited or dangerous activities.

Among these neurotransmitters, DA is involved in the control of appetite and pleasure, including food and sex. Drugs such as cocaine increase the brain levels of DA and can provoke a schizophrenic episode or worsen symptoms of schizophrenia in a patient. Cocaine is also reported to block the reuptake of synaptic dopamine, resulting in increased dopaminergic stimulation and a 'high' feeling. But this process is very complex (O'Brian, p. 1195). Low dopamine (DA) receptor activity seems to enhance heavy drinking, while high levels of this neurotransmitter appear to have a protective effect (Arehart-Treichel 2006b, p. 25).

The endorphin system in the brain is involved in dealing

with pain, promoting pleasure, and managing reaction to stress. Endorphin receptors exist not only in the brain, but also in other parts of the body. During the past 40 years scientists have identified over 60 neurotransmitters. It has been estimated that there are 300 or more naturally produced chemicals in the body which are used by the neurons to send messages from one neuron to another. Neurotransmitters are local messengers that move across synapses to produce certain effects. Hormones are long-distance messengers that are carried by the blood to act on organs distant from the brain (DuPont 1997, pp. 98–104).

Patterns of Drug Consumption

Drugs consumed by users can reach the brain through different routes. Drugs may enter the body through the oral route of administration and be absorbed through the gastrointestinal system. Some drugs are injected directly into the bloodstream. Others enter the body via the respiratory system through smoking or inhalation. Yet a few others like cocaine may be sniffed and are absorbed through the nasal membrane into the blood flow. The most common ways of consuming illicit drugs are through intravenous injection or smoking, both of which result in a faster 'high' experience due to a rapid rise of the drug in the blood and the immediate effect on the brain and pleasure centres. These kinds of drug use have greater addictive power as compared to oral drug use, in which absorption is slower (DuPont 1997, p. 108).

Other Biological Factors

Genetic factors also have been implicated in the development of addiction and alcoholism. Recent scientific research has found that 26 genes and many of the variants of genetic elements located near these genes appear to be implicated in the development of alcoholism and other types of substance abuse (Arehart-Treichel 2006a, p. 25). It has also been reported that early onset of drinking predicts early onset of dependence which may become chronic. Alcoholics also have multiple cases of alcohol dependency in their families.

As alcoholism runs in some families, its inheritance has been meticulously studied on the genetic level. Although alcoholism does not have a single cause, genes play an important role in producing genetic vulnerability to alcohol dependency or protecting against it. It depends on the complex interactions of genes with biological as well as psychosocial factors. Researchers believe that identifying genetic influences on vulnerability to alcoholism can lead to specific treatments. It also helps in educating those at risk to pay attention to their lifestyle. (Nurnberger and Bierut 2007, pp. 47–8).

However, alcohol dependence is an expression of the interaction of multiple genetic and environmental factors. According to Alan Leshner, studies of brain and behaviour have shown that addiction is a biological-behavioural disorder. Its occurrence is due to the effect of prolonged drug use on the brain structure and function. But addiction also involves critical behavioural and social components. Therefore, if addiction is truly a biological-behavioural phenomenon in nature, its treatment should also involve biological, behavioural and social measures for recovery (Leshner, p. 1).

8

PSYCHOSOCIAL FACTORS IN DRUG USE

Among the objectives of civilization should be that of improving the quality of human life and of people's attitudes towards themselves. The present trend in the industrialized world, however, is quite the opposite. According to the writings of the Bahá'í Faith, which unveil the fundamental character of a new world order, 'unless the moral character of a nation is educated, as well as its brain and its talents, civilization has no sure basis' ('Abdu'l-Bahá, *Paris Talks*, p. 21).

The Influence of Lifestyle and Attitude

Let us take a closer look at lifestyles and attitudes in North America, both of which are intimately related to family education. Taking the main causes of mortality in the United States as an example, we find that of the 1.7 million deaths which occur each year in that country, 30 per cent are caused by the consumption of alcohol and tobacco. Use of these two substances by pregnant women often leads to premature birth and subsequent death (300,000 premature births due to tobacco and 200,000 premature births due to alcohol consumption per year (DuPont 1981, p. 268)). A survey conducted by the Centers for Disease Control in Atlanta, Georgia on the leading causes of death in the United States found that '50% of the causative factors were related to lifestyle, 20% [were] related to the environment – mostly to do with occupational exposure, 20% were related to human biology and only 10% were traced to inadequacies of the health care system' (ibid.). Other important factors which contribute to the high death toll in the United States are accidents and suicide. Alcohol and drug use may play an important role in this.

It is interesting to note that improvements in medicine and public health care since 1900 have led to a consistent improvement in general health and a decrease in the death rate of the general population for all age groups in the United States with the exception of young people aged 15–24, who in the past 20 years have experienced a greater rate of mortality than that of 1960 (ibid. p. 267). It has been reported that approximately 50 per cent of all deaths among adolescents in that country result from accidents, predominantly car accidents. Suicide and homicide are the second and third causes of death among adolescents (ibid.). Both these, and probably some of the automobile accidents as well, are closely related to individual attitudes towards life and lifestyle in the modern world.

Drinking and driving

Drugs, particularly alcohol, can impair one's driving ability and skill. Moreover, as drugs affect the reflex system, slowing it down or causing loss of coordination, driving under their influence can be potentially dangerous, especially in an emergency. Individual attention, concentration and judgement are also adversely affected and as a result the likelihood of errors in judgement is increased.

It was estimated that in the 1970s the number of Americans who lost their lives in car accidents in the United States during one year was greater than the number who lost their lives during the entire Vietnam war. Yet that nation was more deeply grieved over its losses in the Vietnam war than it is about the 45,000 deaths and hundreds of thousands of injuries which occur as a result of automobile accidents each year (Cohen 1981b, p. 1). Sidney Cohen (ibid.) has estimated that over one-third of the injuries, and half of the deaths due to accidents, are alcohol-related, and moreover, that 40–60 per cent of single vehicle accidents are due to alcohol intoxication and related effects. There are indications that cannabis can also impair driving performance and cause errors of perception and judgement during driving (ARF 1981, p. 24). With the widespread use of alcohol and cannabis-related substances, particularly among the young, drug-related accidents have become an issue of special concern.

Statistics show that millions of teenagers in the United States drive either their parents' or their own car (Buchan 1977, pp. 12–13). For many, passing a driver's licence exam is like undergoing 'rites of passage' and entering adulthood, and many miscalculate the risk involved in driving. Lowering the age of driving and drinking in some countries has led to tragic consequences. Juvenile deaths caused by car accidents have been climbing at an alarming rate (Ghadirian 1979). In 1977 it was reported that in the United States 60 per cent of these deaths occurred because of drunken driving by teenagers, who are particularly prone to these kinds of tragedy because of inexperience in either driving or drinking.

Substance abuse in the workplace

Substance abuse at the workplace has become a serious concern in recent years. The use of alcohol and drugs in the workplace, particularly in industry and the health professions, can impair judgement and cause accidents which may result in death or disabilities. As an example, from 1975 to 1986 about 50 train accidents were attributed to workers' impairment by the use of alcohol or drugs. 'In those mishaps 37 people were killed, 80 were injured, and more than $34 million worth of property was destroyed' (Castro 1986, p. 41).

The following is another example of substance abuse in the transportation industry.

In September 1984 a pilot for a major international airline called 800-COCAINE, a New Jersey-based hot-line that provides treatment referral and information. He said that he had been up for three days straight snorting cocaine and that he was scheduled to

71

fly a passenger jet to Europe that night. He was feeling exhausted and paranoid, he confided, but was sure he could stay awake and alert if he just kept taking drugs. 'Call in sick and get some sleep,' urged the hot-line counselor. The counselor, who never found out what the pilot finally decided to do, says that such calls are not unusual (ibid.).

Among substances of abuse, alcohol, marijuana and cocaine are the most widely consumed in the workplace. Drugs are taken for various reasons, ranging from the desire to experience over-alertness (in the case of business executives and athletes) to the need to alleviate tension and tedium. Whatever the motive, these substances affect personal judgement, perception, competence and quality of performance. Their use among health professionals has been a matter of particular concern. It has been estimated (Keeve 1984) that up to 15 per cent of international physicians are professionally impaired as a result of alcoholism and drug abuse.

More than any other ailment, alcoholism causes absenteeism, high medical expense and reduced work quality. According to North Carolina's Research Triangle Institute, it was estimated that alcoholism cost the United States economy $117 billion in 1983. With this amount of money, the country could build schools, hospitals and save the lives of thousands of people around the world who die of hunger each year.

The work environment can influence alcohol and drug consumption. Psychosocial and cultural as well as economic factors play a role in the process. For example, the workers in the vineyards of Western Cape Province, South Africa, were offered free wine: a man would receive a bottle a day and his wife half that amount. Although this practice is presently illegal, research suggests that it continues in 20 per cent of the farms in Western Cape (*Globe* 1999a, p. 2).

The purpose of keeping the workers addicted to alcohol was to avoid paying them decent wages. As women were affected by the free alcohol, so were their children who developed foetal alcohol syndrome. Eleven per cent of the farmworkers' children were affected by this disease (ibid).

In the United States, the US Department of Labor has estimated that up to 9 million workers use drugs and that employees who abuse drugs and alcohol have 66 per cent more absences from the job and file more compensation claims than non-abusers. Such drug or alcohol abuse is also involved in 50 per cent of all workplace accidents and abusers use 300 per cent more health benefits than other employees (ILO 2006, pp. 33–34).

A survey by Portman Group in the United Kingdom showed that 63 per cent of employees phone in sick after getting drunk the night before instead of coming to work (ibid). In Alberta, Canada, alcohol and drug misuse costs US$ 400 million annually in lost productivity (ibid. p. 34).

Society and Human Values

All this is a clear indication that progress in science and technology and the resulting increase in material wealth do not necessarily bring greater awareness of moral values or a positive lifestyle. It is in these areas that moral belief and education are most important. Here the science of medicine and the values of religion can meet with the common purpose of improving human life as in ancient times, and particularly in Greece, when a physician was also a priest who treated both the visible and invisible wounds of body and soul.

Modern civilization has increased human expectations of comfort and security. These expectations have penetrated deeply into the habits and attitudes of nations and affected their traditional values. Never before have human beings advanced so rapidly in discovering ways and means to appease their psychosocial needs, to relieve their pain and anxiety. As testimony to this we witness on the one hand the enormous synthesis and rapid dissemination of various types of mood and mind-altering substances such as psychedelic drugs and stimulants and, on the other hand, the increasing popularity of relaxation techniques, whether imported from the east or invented in the west. The increasing recognition of the problem of stress has also stimulated new efforts and research into ways of coping with the wear and tear of life and has begun a new era in human adaptation to stressful environments. Medicine, which was traditionally concerned primarily with the art of healing physical ailments, is now challenged to produce remedies for the invisible wounds of the human mind and soul and to break through fear and despair. The response of the medical world has been overwhelming: through various types of chemical substances we can now alleviate fear and anxiety or excite the depressed and apathetic mood. We can stimulate or inhibit the appetite, tame a violent temper or change a person's perception of the world around him. Not all drugs, however, have positive effects on the mind and body. Through the use of some drugs, reason, the most precious gift bestowed upon man, can be altered or totally distorted. From a previously meek individual, a monster of violence and destruction can be unleashed.

Lifestyles based on gratification

In the western world considerable emphasis is placed on the necessity of sensory satisfaction in daily life. This over-consciousness of the gratification of the senses has further heightened sensitivity to pain and frustration. Quick relief from any kind of discomfort has become part of our notion of health. Pain and suffering are considered abnormal or unacceptable conditions, while pleasure and comfort are sought after as indispensable necessities. Well-being is seen as health in the absence of pain and discomfort, rather than health with the ability to cope with pain and distress. Western society has achieved remarkable skills is controlling the environment through modern technology. With the advance of science, this will to control has extended from without to within the person. Hence, by means of various drugs, certain internal wants and impulses are inhibited while others are stimulated.

This lifestyle is continuously nurtured and reinforced through social contacts and by the news media, particularly television. Furthermore, because of the very competitive and achievement-oriented aspects of present-day society, the individual also dreads failure. In such circumstances a search for seemingly comforting agents such as alcohol and psychoactive drugs may begin.

Consumption of these substances temporarily gratifies the internal need for security, but at the same time masks the individual's painful realization of his failure to solve his problems, thereby further delaying growth and maturity. When psychological or spiritual distress is removed without the attainment of any insight into its meaning, certain experiences essential for growth fail to take place. Without such learning experiences an individual cannot achieve his full potential or fulfil his purpose in living. Parents should instead educate their children to welcome the tests and difficulties of life as new opportunities for learning, rather than deny them by means of psychological or biochemical manipulation.

To explore this matter further, I introduce Figure 3 which

Figure 3
Abnormal response in a self-centred individual

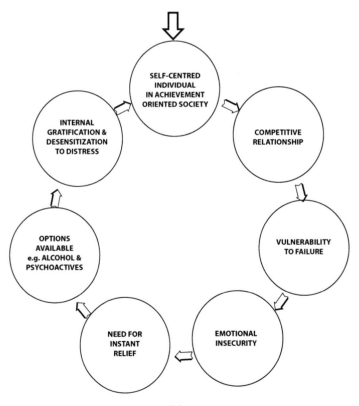

illustrates the phases that a self-centred individual goes through in relation to an intensely competitive social structure. The self-centred individual in our analysis here refers to someone who is more self-oriented than other-oriented. Such an individual, living in an achievement-oriented society, enters into a competitive relationship with others. This competition is encouraged by the social systems to which he belongs. The continuous struggle to maintain an idealized self-image in a competitive relationship diminishes his tolerance of failure and renders him vulnerable to stressful situations. Unable to accept the reality of failure and to cope with the distress it generates, he is forced to seek other ways of coping with what is essentially a moral dilemma.

Coping with the stresses of life takes different forms, depending on the individual. For some it becomes a creative process, while for others it leads to destructive behaviour. If alcohol and psychoactive drugs are available, they may seem to an insecure individual a convenient way of providing relief. But by choosing this option he only wards off the fear and anxiety of failure without solving the underlying problem. As a result, the vicious circle continues without any insight being achieved.

Mankind today is going through a worldwide period of crisis in its development, a crisis which has an important effect on the spread of the use of drugs. In many respects, this crisis is similar to that faced by adolescents before maturity is reached. Like an adolescent, mankind has left behind childhood and the dark age of ignorance. It has entered a stage where competition, self-centredness, unpredictability and the need for a new identity are intensely felt. Intellectual and material progress have reached a high level in many countries, but this progress has not brought peace and security. On the contrary, the spread of lawlessness and violence, the expansion of conventional and nuclear weapons, the contamination of the atmosphere of the earth and the pollution of the environment, the breakdown of the family and of traditional institutions, and the crisis in science, religion, ethics and education suggest a rapid disintegration of the old world order. The increase in alcoholism, drug use and suicide are further indicators of accelerating tension and confusion. To Bahá'ís, these developments herald the collapse of a deficient system that is ultimately to be replaced by a new world order and a new civilization. But for humanity at large they are very distressing signs which further contribute to the complexity of the widespread problem of drug use and alcoholism.

From freedom to fear

Many substance abusers have their own concept of freedom and contest the rules and values of society. They believe that, as adults, they are in sole possession of themselves and can do to their bodies and minds whatever they please. Ironically, the ultimate destiny of alcoholics or drug addicts is the loss of that very freedom they value so highly. They soon realize that the body acquires a physical tolerance as it becomes dependent on a drug, meaning that a larger amount of the substance is required in order to achieve the same result. An additional realization is that failure to obtain the needed drug within a certain length of time produces a psycho-physiological withdrawal reaction which can be both painful and dangerous, depending on the nature and potency of the drug. The addict is, of course, highly aware that, by virtue of this dependency, he has left himself open to undesirable consequences. Thus, he faces two moral dilemmas:

1. He has lost his freedom to be himself. His brain and behaviour are affected by alcohol or drugs and he is no longer in full command of himself. As a result, his reasoning may be impoverished and his behaviour may become volatile or absurd. Moreover, by becoming dependent on a lifeless, speechless, and indifferent chemical agent with which he cannot even communicate, he has subjected himself to the constant fear of withdrawal symptoms. The anguish of withdrawal, in the event of failure to obtain the addictive substance, may be so intense that the primary objective of achieving pleasure eventually loses its meaning, especially if the addict has no financial security. Pleasure is replaced by fear in a perpetual struggle for existence, and dreams of discovering the serenity of nirvana are changed into nightmares of 'chemical slavery'.

As Shakespeare wrote in *Othello* (II.iii):

> O thou invisible spirit of wine! If thou hast no name to be known by, let us call thee devil! . . . O God! That man should put an enemy in their mouths to steal away their brains . . .

2. In an effort to avoid a possible withdrawal reaction, the addicted person may find it necessary to obtain the drug on which he is dependent by any possible means. The rules of ethics and the governing laws of society may have to be broken in order to achieve this goal. Breaking and entering, robbery, violence, and even murder may be the unfortunate consequences of this. The addicted victim, caught in his desperate predicament, and possibly suffering from impaired judgement, may endanger his own life unless psychiatric help is sought.

Drug-induced violence and aggressive behaviour have been widely reported in medical literature and the media.

One study (Fauman and Fauman 1979) suggests that chronic use of phencylidine (PCP) can cause violent behaviour directed towards the self or others. According to the researchers, this violent behaviour was inconsistent with the behaviour of the users while not under the influence of this drug. In one report there was a case of murder and self-mutilation under the influence of PCP. This and other observations suggested that badly impaired reasoning provoked reckless behaviour which could be fatal. For example, one PCP user was found climbing into a polar bear cage to take a photograph.

In view of the fact that the use of alcohol and drugs of any kind is largely motivated by a number of psychological and social factors, Table 2 shows a summary of these contributing factors.

Pleasure without purpose

Pleasure can be obtained in many different ways. It can be experienced through intellectual achievements, artistic creativity or physical and other activities. Whatever the means, the feeling is the same. For a mystic, the spiritual realization of his unity with the

Table 2

Some important factors that contribute to adolescent alcohol and drug use

1. Childhood education
2. Peer group influence
3. Parental identity model (i.e. parental alcoholism)
4. Culturally and socially permissive attitude or habits (i.e. use of alcohol or drugs)
5. Social incentives: acceptability, availability and advertising of substances, e.g. through the media
6. Family conflicts and poor communication at home
7. Rejection of parental and social values
8. Personal will to pleasure: 'to feel better'
9. Alienation
10. Loneliness, shyness and deprivation of affection
11. Feeling of personal failure or despair (particularly in a competitive society)
12. Boredom and apathy
13. Aggressive impulses
14. Search for personal identity
15. Search for escape
16. Social isolation or over-stimulation
17. Lack of spiritual or religious values
18. Search for a rite of passage and symbolic expression of adulthood
19. Conscious or subconscious self-destructive motives
20. Curiosity and desire to experiment
21. Emotional or social stress
22. Inability to accept oneself
23. Craving for a drug already addicted to
24. Absence of positive alternatives
25. Depression or other mental disorders.

universe becomes a source of joy and rapture even though materially he may be in dire straits. In all these cases, pleasure is earned through personal effort, often involving sacrifice of individual comfort. Drug-induced pleasure is not earned and there is no goal or purpose beyond that of simply experiencing gratification. Thus gratification, which is for some the spontaneous outcome of purposeful activity, may become in others the guiding principle of a hedonistic drive.

On the individual level, a precedence of sense orientation over insight orientation has been found among drug users in contemporary North American culture. In a study of adolescent drug users in 1972, Scott (1972, p. 48) reported that when the subjects were asked: 'What do you think you are getting out of drugs?', 69 per cent responded, 'Experiencing more' (meaning feeling better). Only 1 per cent believed that they learned something about themselves. This further supports the view that over-emphasis on sensual satisfaction often plays an important role in the motives for drug use.

Pleasure consciousness seems to have left its mark on the vocabulary of drug users in identifying their favourite psychoactive substances. Among the psychedelics, the following are a few examples: *Cannabis sativa* (a plant, the active chemical ingredient of which is THC – tetrahydrocannabinol) is also known among other names as 'dope', 'bhang', 'kif', 'pot', 'ganja', and 'grass'. LSD (lysergic acid diethylamide) is referred to as 'acid', 'trips', or 'sunshine', while STP (or DOM; 2.5-dimethoxy, 4-methylamphetamine) stands for 'serenity-tranquillity-and-peace-pill'. The plant *Ipomoea violacea* is called 'morning glory seeds'. PCP (phencylidine) is widely known as 'angel dust'.

Among the psycho-stimulants ('uppers') cocaine is referred to as 'happy trails' and 'heaven leaf', while Methadrin is sometimes identified as 'speed' and 'crank'. Among the psycho-depressants ('downers') such as barbiturates, Seco-barbital capsules are called 'red devils'; Nembutal, 'yellow jackets'; and Amytal, 'blue heavens' and 'blue dolls' (Inaba et al. 1977, pp. 16–27). Morphine, the principal ingredient of opium, is also a psycho-depressant drug and derives its name from the Greek god Morpheus, the god of dreams.

Not all substance abuse occurs as a result of hedonistic drives

80

and self-centredness, nor is this problem confined to the western world. A substantial number of individuals, especially adults, may use drugs as a response to their anxiety and despair or, following a chronic illness, may make non-medical use of prescriptions.

Sidney Cohen, one of the leading authorities on the problem of alcoholism and drug abuse in America, identified some of the causes of drug abuse in society as follows (1971, pp. 547–50):

1. The attenuation of established values without the appearance of new and more suitable values to replace them.

2. The decay of the traditional customs and beliefs that used to bind groups of people together, e.g. religion *(religio:* to bind together), family ties and the common roots of national, ethnic and tribal allegiances.

3. The decline in visible and viable aspirations for many.

4. The persistence of an 'effluent society' in our midst, with its diseases of hopelessness and poor self-esteem; the rise of an 'affluent society', with its diseases of directionlessness.

5. The inadequacy of our educational system, with its unbalanced emphasis on training the intellect with only minimal attention paid to training the senses and the emotions.

For the younger generation, we have seen other important elements involved in alcohol and drug use – the desire for adventure and the quest for novel experiences in a dull or indifferent social climate. Some adolescents may use drugs as a means of combatting boredom and depression, while others do so to cope with a sense of alienation and disillusionment.

Today, the easy availability of natural or synthetic stimulants allows almost anyone to manipulate the pleasure centres in his brain and indulge in some sort of artificial gratification and elation. In such circumstances pleasure loses its meaning and is no longer a reward for survival.

Lawrence Hatterer wrote, 'Addictive behaviour has invaded every aspect of American life today. We all feel the cloud of concern about becoming addictive – preoccupation with weight, smoking, drinking too much, or being caught in an excess of spending, acquiring, gambling, sex or work . . . Ours is a society of polarized excesses that is the essence of addictive life' (p. 15). He goes on to say that in this process,

> the person has an overpowering desire or need for a substance, object, action, interaction, or fantasy or milieu that produces a psychophysiologic reaction – a 'high'. This reaction is sought repetitively, impulsively, and compulsively. At first it is felt as a pleasurable way to cope with a psychic conflict or stress that has caused conscious or unconscious pain that seems intolerable. In the early stages of the process, one feels partial or total relief. There is a false sense of resolving conflict or stress because it is masked or extinguished by psychic and/or physical pleasure. This pleasure diminishes as the process continues; one feels less relief, less sense of coping or resolution . . . (pp. 16–17).

Scientists using animals to explore the nature of self-induced pleasure have found that cocaine, for example, is a potent chemical reinforcer of pleasure for which animals are willing to labour strenuously, ignoring the most basic drives. 'In an unlimited access situation,' Sidney Cohen explains,

> monkeys will self-administer cocaine by bar-pressing [pressing down a lever] for it until they die in status epilecticus. In one study, primates bar-pressed 12,800 times in order to a get a single dose of cocaine. They will work for cocaine in preference to food even though they are starving. They will continue to bar-press even though a receptive female is in their cage. They will prefer an electric shock in order to obtain a large dose of cocaine despite the fact that they could have received a lesser dose without a shock (1981c, p. 1).

Presumably, if humans likewise had unlimited access to cocaine,

82

they would react similarly in order to obtain the drug. For a human being to experience pleasure, the information he receives from the environment must stimulate the pleasure centres of his brain. This makes the experience of the sensation of pleasure possible (Jones and Jones 1977, p. 16). Under normal circumstances, the desired information reaches the brain through the pathway of the senses or through the thoughts, memory and imagination. The pathway between the information received and the pleasure centres in the brain is not clear, but the pleasure centres are believed to be located in the limbic region of the brain (ibid. p. 17). This region plays a very important role in the expression of emotion, retention of memory, control of the autonomic nervous system and the control of drives, including those of a sexual nature. In primitive man the limbic region was the centre for the instincts of survival, and in modern man it is considered to be the thinking brain (ibid. p. 16). Its role in pleasure has been the subject of extensive investigation by scientists. In one experiment it was reported that

> using laboratory animals, permanent electrodes were implanted in the limbic region of the brain, and the animals were then trained to stimulate this area by activating a lever that caused a mild, nerve stimulating electrical current to pass between the electrodes. During this training, the animals quickly established a pattern of frequent self-stimulation. Unless stopped, they continued to stimulate themselves until they dropped from exhaustion, and after sleeping they would immediately start pressing the lever. Even if they had been without food and water, they would choose the lever for brain stimulation rather than levers they knew provided food or water (ibid. p. 17).

In a similar manner, most abused substances cause euphoric moods to varying degrees (see Table 3). Such feelings of elation may give users a false sense of their own well-being, strength and power, while in fact they may be weak, sick, and helpless.

It is believed that when the pleasure centres of the brain are stimulated repeatedly through chemical substances they lose their natural sensitivity to such stimuli. This explains the inability of

Table 3
Some pharmacological properties of abused drugs

Drug Class	Example	Euphoria	Psychological Dependence	Tolerance	Withdrawal Syndrome
Narcotics	**Heroin**	+++	+++	+++	+++
Sedatives	**Barbiturates**	++	+++	++	+++
Anaesthetics	**Alcohol**	++	+++	++	+++
	Toluene	++	++	+	(+)
Anxiolytics	**Diazepam**	++	++	+	+
	Meprobamate	++	++	++	++
Hallucinogens	**LSD**	++	+	+++	-
	THC	++	++	++	(+)
Stimulants	**Amphetamines**	+++	+++	++	+
	Cocaine	+++	+++	-	-
Ganglionic stimulants	**Tobacco**	(+)	++	++	+

Source: S. Cohen 1976, p. 3. Reprinted with permission.

some chronic drug users to derive the same level of pleasure out of drug use over the course of time. Hardin Jones, a renowned medical physiologist from the University of California at Berkeley, who has done extensive studies on the physiological effect of drugs on the brain and the nervous system, believes that when a drug user

derives pleasure from a drug, he is getting pleasure from his brain's mechanism, which is artificially activated by the drug. When the pleasure mechanism is not allowed to operate on its natural terms – when it is abused by drugs – it begins to fail, so that the pleasurable sensations are weakened. Ultimately they may become imperceptible. The person is then sensually deprived. The mechanisms can recover, however, and again become sensitive to the natural sources of stimulation, which can give pleasure without harming the mechanism. Restoration of the pleasure mechanism is the key to rehabilitation from drug abuse (Jones and Jones 1977, p. 8).

Pleasure which is induced artificially, is not directed toward a goal, or bears no meaning (as in the case of drugs) is 'a trick played on the brain' (Cohen 1981c, p. 3) with undesirable consequences yet to be explored by medicine.

In search of happiness

Happiness, that elusive state, has been sought after throughout the ages at all levels of society. The search for it is particularly intense in societies where one finds a greater reliance on material means and power as a source of security. In such societies happiness is perceived as an elixir to be found and cherished forever. Affected by a materialistic view of life and desperately trying to be happy whatever the cost, people will be greatly attracted by stimulants and other mood-altering drugs.

Chemical 'happiness' is made available for sale and public consumption. This 'happiness' may take different shapes and forms: powder, pill, liquid, glue, or inhalant. These chemical messengers of 'happiness' have been hailed by their lovers as 'angel dust', 'morning glory', 'happy trails', 'crack', 'red devils', 'designer drugs' and so on. Others are served frequently in elegant glasses with such exotic names as 'bloody mary', 'pink lady', 'bloody caesar', 'black russian', and 'stinger'. These, and many more yet to be discovered, are the commercial faces of 'happiness' in many parts of the world.

In this scenario, 'happiness' becomes a commodity which can be obtained at the store, carried home in a bottle and served at a party. It can be mailed to a remote area or sold in the street or black market (Cohen 1982). It can be traded, bargained for, or invested in. Such 'happiness' can be blown away by a gentle wind or washed away by the rain. It can become a cause of accidents, war, violence and bloodshed. 'Happiness' of this kind can be consumed by smoking, drinking, sniffing or injecting. It may appear in the form of a lifeless white powder carried by a frail-looking youth who wants to be inspired by it, kneels before it, supplicates to it and inhales it in a quiet part of a school or in a deserted corner of a street. It may appear as a glass of wine to a despondent man who has lost his job or to a woman who finds no other way out of her loneliness. 'Happiness' may be a pale-coloured liquid to inject into one's arm to excite the brain. 'Happiness', by this definition, can be synthesized in a chemist's laboratory or may be made in a brewery. It can be planted in the backyard or it can be cultivated on farms. The vast plains of countries such as Afghanistan, Turkey and India and the hills and mountains of Colombia, Mexico, and Bolivia, for example, are rich in cultivated 'happiness'! Yet people of some of these countries are among the poorest in the world. Today in many countries farmers cultivate the seeds of illusive 'happiness' such as opium poppy, coca, and marijuana, rather than the seeds of rice and wheat, as the former are more profitable. Companies and private enterprises export these products to many unhappy people around the world and invest the millions of dollars of profits. Governments too have vested interest in the revenue from these products. This kind of 'happiness' has become an incorporated enterprise to serve the restless and unhappy people of this planet.

In a world where human values and feelings are defined and measured in terms of their material importance and use, happiness has lost its true meaning. In such a climate, happiness is sought through the use of substances which stimulate pleasure and invoke a state of joy and ecstasy. Such autogenic and artificial 'happiness' has no place in the realm of human reality that perceives joy as a normal response of the mind and soul to a particular environmental experience or inner enlightenment. Drug-induced joy is a deceptive experience which can only delay the natural course of human growth and fulfilment. Drug-free happiness is not only possible, but also very desirable for personal growth and well-being.

Happiness can be experienced by anyone; it is our attitude towards life and its purpose which plays the most important role in its development. True happiness is closely related to man's spiritual reality. The Bahá'í concept of happiness and progress is based on man's relationship with his Creator. In this relationship, man evolves and progresses by drawing closer to Almighty God. Happiness is closely associated with this process of evolution ('Abdu'l-Bahá, *Secret of Divine Civilization*, p. 60). Indeed, 'human happiness is founded upon spiritual behaviour' ('Abdu'l-Bahá, *Selections*, p. 127).

'Abdu'l-Bahá describes two kinds of happiness. 'As to material happiness,' He states,

> it never exists; nay, it is but imagination, an image reflected in mirrors, a spectre and shadow. Consider the nature of material happiness. It is something which but slightly removes one's afflictions; yet the people imagine it to be joy, delight, exultation and blessing. All the material blessings, including food, drink, etc. tend only to allay thirst, hunger and fatigue. They bestow no delight on the mind nor pleasure on the soul; nay, they furnish only the bodily wants. So this kind of happiness has no real existence. As to spiritual happiness, this is the true basis of the life of man, for life is created for happiness, not for sorrow; for pleasure, not for grief . . . Spiritual happiness is life eternal. This is a light which is not followed by darkness. This is an honour which is not followed by shame . . . (quoted in Hyde Paine 1944, pp. 17–18).

H.B. Danesh (1986) identified four distinct circumstances in which happiness is experienced:

1. The most common condition which brings about happiness is the gratification of basic human needs such as food, shelter, sex and physical comfort. The author recognizes the fact that human happiness goes far beyond satisfaction of physical needs and desires.

2. The second condition conducive to happiness is the fulfilment of the individual needs to be respected, accepted and loved by others.

3. The third common cause of happiness, he believes, is human accomplishment. To fulfil this task, two conditions need to be met: 'The first is the existence of a harmony of thought, feeling, and action, while the second is the dedication of these thoughts, feelings and actions to the development of our true selves as spiritual and noble beings' (p. 23).

4. The fourth and the highest form of happiness is the one which arises from man's relationship with his Creator and which inspires him in his creativity (pp. 23–4).

Among these conditions of happiness the first one is the most elementary form. In fact, what is referred to in this analysis as happiness, in reality, is mere 'imagination'. It is a condition in which some of the basic human needs such as thirst and hunger are satisfied and this satisfaction is perpetuated throughout physical life. It is different from other kinds of happiness. Alcohol and drugs, although used to achieve a higher level of happiness such as acceptance of one's self, in reality interact with a human being's most elementary physical needs and instinctual drives. Their effects are like the reflection of a mirage which will swiftly vanish from the mind. I believe that the most evolved and praiseworthy form of happiness, besides the one which emanates from an individual's relationship with God, is the joy and happiness of serving humanity and transforming narcissistic self-interest into an altruistic attitude in one's love for mankind.

In search of meaning in life

In human nature there is an evolutionary process at work which has a transforming effect. It goes beyond the pleasure and pain principle. To tap this precious inner reality, one needs to be connected to a higher level of consciousness and the knowledge of the ultimate purpose and meaning of life. This requires access to a system of education which is based on spiritual values as well as scientific understanding of human nature.

The Bahá'í teachings encourage the discovery of an inner source of peace and delight which each one of us potentially possesses. It recognizes happiness as a natural outcome of man's quest for the realization of his purpose in life. True joy of life emanates from one's love of and longing for reunion with his Creator – like a lover whose true moment of rapture and delight is when he is reunited with his beloved.

With the organic growth of human society and the advent

of the age of maturity there will come a day when we shall leave behind this adolescent stage of adventure-seeking, risk-taking, and searching. We shall find a new vision of life and the universe and a novel approach to joy and contentment. There will be a greater spiritual orientation toward the joy of life than the present material drive for pleasure. In that stage of development, people will not poison their brain in order to draw pleasure from it nor will they humiliate their intelligence as a trade-off for excitement. There will be a true concept of joy and the perception of happiness. Excitement and intoxication will be in abundance, but of a different nature. These will be the excitements of a mature age and with different meanings: the delight of acquiring the attributes of God and the ecstasy of discovering the truth about the mysteries of life. One will experience blissful delight from reaching a new level of consciousness. The cup of human contentment will be filled with the knowledge of God and remembrance of Him. There will be intoxication too, but with the celestial wine of love of God and of all humanity. Joy will be felt as a result of serving mankind and upholding the banners of peace and justice. None of these excitements and ecstasies will be exclusive to any privileged class of society nor will they tax anyone financially. They will not appear as a result of shooting a substance into the veins nor from inhaling a toxic preparation. They will not burn out the brain cells, freeze the judgement, poison the body or impoverish the reason. They will not cause physical dependence, nor will they lead to hangovers or withdrawal symptoms! They will not be cultivated in a vineyard, purchased from the store, or secretly seached out for consumption. There will be no need to guard against their illicit trafficking. They will be the natural expressions of human growth and coming of age.

The mystic character of inner joy and serenity which one may attain in this world can be discerned throughout the Bahá'í writings. The Báb, the Herald Messenger of the Bahá'í Faith, prays: 'Cheer our hearts through the potency of Thy love and good-pleasure and bestow upon us steadfastness that we may willingly submit to Thy Will and Thy Decree' (*Selections*, p. 214). 'Abdu'l-Bahá writes in one of His prayers: 'O God, my God! Fill up for me the cup of detachment from all things, and in the assembly of Thy splendours and bestowals, rejoice me with the wine of loving Thee' (*Bahá'í Prayers*, p. 57). Elsewhere, 'Abdu'l-Bahá describes human honour and happiness in these words: '. . . man's supreme honour and real happiness lie in self-respect, in high resolves and noble purposes, in integrity and moral quality, in immaculacy of mind' (*Secret of Divine Civilization*, p. 19). Again He states: 'The soul of man must be happy no matter where he is. One must attain to that condition of inward beatitude and peace, then outward circumstances will not alter his spiritual calmness and joyousness' (ibid.).

9

EFFECTS OF SUBSTANCE ABUSE

The Dynamics of Physiological Dependence

Some drug use may result in psychological dependence, while other drugs may lead to physiological dependence. Drug addiction is a term which usually refers to a state of physiological dependence characterized by the development of tolerance to consumption of the drug. In such a state, a sudden cessation of the drug will provoke a withdrawal (abstinence) syndrome. Substances such as the opium alkaloid morphine cause physical dependence, while drugs like amphetamines and cannabis produce psychological dependence.

It is believed that the marijuana currently being sold and used is ten times more potent than previous supplies and therefore its THC (tetrahydrocannabinol) concentration is stronger. Furthermore, it is now more likely to be mixed with other drugs which increases the seriousness of its adverse effects on the central nervous system. THC is a fat-soluble component and possesses a half-life of three days. This is the period of time when the drug is active in the blood circulation. Consequently, marijuana consumption is associated with concentration of the potent THC component in the brain, liver, lungs, reproductive organs and other systems (Sanders 1982, p. 12). The effects of this substance on human behaviour are outlined below.

The synthetic forms of drugs are prepared either through modification of the chemical structure of drugs from natural sources or through the synthetic preparation of related components. Drugs in the former group include LSD (from ergot, obtained from a fungus) and heroin (Jones and Jones 1977, pp. 30–31).

The chemical substances, after being absorbed into the blood stream, are transported to various organs, including the brain. The limbic region of the brain is particularly sensitive to the effects of psychoactive compounds (ibid. pp. 35–7).

Drugs can alter the activities of the autonomic nervous system. The physiological pathways of the brain may be thrown out of balance due to the consumption of drugs such as heroin. Pulse and blood pressure may drop, the body temperature decline, vision become less accurate, the perception of pain may be reduced, and the mind become clouded (ibid. pp. 37–8). The brain contains small blood vessels called capillaries which are very numerous (if they were placed end to end, their length would measure about 100 miles). However, at any one time they contain less than one teaspoon of blood (ibid. p. 33). These very fine brain vessels carry oxygen enzymes and nutrient substances vital for the survival and functioning of the brain cells. In the case of drug and alcohol consumption, these capillaries carry toxic substances which will have adverse effects on the natural functioning of the brain cells and the hormones of the central nervous system. Consequently, abnormal behaviours will be manifested; these are briefly illustrated in Table 4.

In medicine any drug, besides having certain specific beneficial effects, exerts a number of undesirable side effects. If a drug is not prescribed properly, its dangers may outweigh its therapeutic effects. Alcohol and other psychoactive substances affect various systems and their functions directly or indirectly. Although their main effect is on the brain and its functions, other systems such as the respiratory and cardiovascular systems are also affected as they are closely interrelated.

Table 4
The effects of psychoactive substances on mind and mood

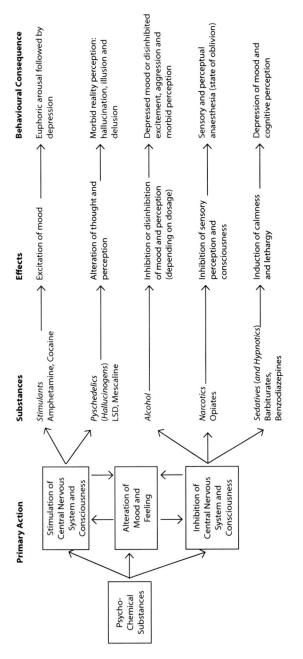

Primary Action	Substances	Effects	Behavioural Consequence
Stimulation of Central Nervous System and Consciousness	*Stimulants* Amphetamine, Cocaine	Excitation of mood	Euphoric arousal followed by depression
Alteration of Mood and Feeling	*Pyschedelics (Hallucinogens)* LSD, Mescaline	Alteration of thought and perception	Morbid reality perception: hallucination, illusion and delusion
	Alcohol	Inhibition or disinhibition of mood and perception (depending on dosage)	Depressed mood or disinhibited excitement, aggression and morbid perception
Inhibition of Central Nervous System and Consciousness	*Narcotics* Opiates	Inhibition of sensory perception and consciousness	Sensory and perceptual anaesthesia (state of oblivion)
	Sedatives (and Hypnotics) Barbiturates, Benzodiazepines	Induction of calmness and lethargy	Depression of mood and cognitive perception

Psycho-Chemical Substances

Note: Most of these substances cause addiction and depression.

Characteristics and effects of 'ecstasy'

Popular notions and perceptions about synthetic amphetamine-type substances include the image of their being modern, relatively benign, fashionable, clean and socially acceptable. Ecstasy users rarely regard themselves as drug addicts.

Intrinsic characteristics of ATS that influence consumer preference are reported to include their special properties, which provide empathy, self-confidence, alertness, endurance, better physical performance and an anorectic effect, its different forms (ATS can be smoked, sniffed, inhaled, ingested or injected), the duration of their CNS stimulant effect which is longer than that of cocaine, their bioavailability which is higher than that of cocaine, their particular pharmacological profiles which can provide stimulant, hallucinogenic, and entactogenic effects and their low cost and easy domestic availability. (UN 1996, p. 119) However, depending on a person's cultural beliefs, expectations, state of mind, and genetic make-up, the adverse effects of ecstasy can vary, for example, from experiencing paranoia to sleep deprivation, disinhibition and other disorders stated below.

MDMA experienced at raves has a somewhat different effect from MDMA taken in quiet surroundings. The combination of the drug with music and dancing produces an exhilarating trance-like state, perhaps similar to that experienced in tribal rituals or religious ceremonies. It increases awareness of touch and sound.

People who normally enjoy ecstasy can also sometimes experience hallucinations (though this may be due to the effect of another drug such as LSD sold as ecstasy) and paranoia. (Saunders 1993). Pleasurable effects decrease with frequent use, while undesirable side effects increase with both larger doses and frequency of use (Solowij et al. 1992).

Ecstasy can affect two neurotransmission systems: dopamine – which stimulates the organism (accelerated heart-rate, diminution of fatigue) and serotonin – which is responsible for the empathogenic effects (sense of conviability, removal of inhibition) (PEDDRO 1998, pp. 12–14). Dysfunction of the central serotonergic system has been linked with depression, suicide and aggressive behaviours and with impairments in cognitive functions and mood regulation (Steele et al. 1994). Since MDMA has the ability to affect the serotonergic system, the possibility of psychiatric disturbances exists (O'Connor 1994).

Depression (Bennazzi and Mazzoli 1991), panic attacks (Whitaker-Azmitia and Aronson 1989) and flashbacks of frightening visual illusions have been reported after consumption of MDMA. Curran et al. (1997) in a study investigating the effect of weekend use of MDMA on mood and cognitive functioning found that the 'high' at the weekend may lead to a 'low' mid-week and to attention problems.

The major risk associated with ecstasy is dehydration and hyperthermia (PEDDRO pp. 12–14). Spontaneous intracerebral haemorrhage has been described following ecstasy ingestion (Harries and De Silva 1992). In addition, MDMA has been shown to affect liver function and may cause liver failure in some individuals. Hepatotoxicity can occur from a single or multiple exposures to MDMA (Henry et al. 1992).

Since ecstasy is a relatively new phenomenon, the long-term implications of its use are still unknown. Nevertheless, MDMA is not the harmless drug that its users perceive it to be. Other documented adverse effects of MDMA ingestion include cardiac arrhythmia and hepatotoxicity, heart attack and fatalities. MDMA has also been shown to precipitate neurological and psychiatric conditions. Some of these risks associated with ecstasy may be linked with pre-existing psychological, neurological or physical problems (PEDDRO 1998, pp. 12–14).

Effects on Mind and Mood

The effect of any substance on the mind and mood depends on the following factors: the nature and potency of the substance, the quantity consumed and the personality, predisposition and emotional state of the individual.

The psychoactive effects of drugs can be divided into two groups (Cohen 1976, p. 1) as follows: those that alter mind and consciousness, and those that alter mood and feelings (Table 4).

1. *Consciousness* is an important function of the human mind; it includes perception, comprehension and preparation for reaction to external or internal events or stimuli. In medical practice the perceptual capacity of consciousness may need to be altered, for example, to avoid pain during a surgical operation, or its focus may be shifted by means of psychological suggestion as in hypnosis. Among the substances which lower the level of consciousness and inhibit sensory perception, especially of pain, are opiates, such as morphine and heroin. Consumption of either drug will result in a state of passive pleasure, diminution of consciousness and oblivion from the surrounding world – a perceptual anaesthesia.

Another form of drug-induced alteration of mind and consciousness is the stimulation of sensory perception. Hallucinogenic drugs such as LSD can cause these experiences.

Under the influence of drugs, the individual's sensitivity and responsiveness to the environment change. Disturbance of the stimulus-response process occurs not only in physiological activities, but also in psychological relationships. According to Hardin Jones and his associates (1977), the use of most of the psychoactive drugs, especially the hallucinogens, upsets the chemical balance of the communication and response mechanisms in the brain. Moreover, due to the disruption of control centres, some unreal and distorted images are produced and the perception of some of the senses, such as hearing and smell, are upset. The interpretation of information received by the brain may become distorted so that colour can be 'heard', and smell and sound can be 'seen'. Drugs can alter not only sensory information, but also its interpretation by the brain.

It is recorded in an Arabic story (Kline 1977, p. 4) that three travellers, an alcoholic, an opium addict and a hashish user, arrived at a city after nightfall when the gates of the city had been closed. The alcoholic shouted, 'Let us bang on the gates until someone is aroused.' The opium addict murmured, 'Perhaps we should all lie down and sleep quietly until morning.' The hashish user whispered his alternative suggestion, 'Let us slip in through the keyhole.' This tale shows how different drugs can affect human behaviour differently.

Jones (p. 50) reported that drugs such as alcohol and marijuana lower the inhibiting capacity of the brain (repression of the instinctual drives and emotional impulses). The loss or reduction of inhibition is directly related to the extent of intoxication. As a result, a state of disinhibition and release of impulsive behaviour may follow, due to the disturbance in the control system of the frontal lobe of the brain.

2. *Alteration of mood* is one of the major reasons for drug use. This alteration may be aimed either at evoking pleasurable feeling and euphoria, or obtaining relief from unpleasant or depressive moods. In the pursuit of these changes of mood, an abnormal cycle of perpetual drug use and addiction may be established. Individuals who are basically insecure and socially unfulfilled and who have not achieved adequate skills in problem-solving and coping mechanisms are more vulnerable to chemical dependency in which substances replace the real solution.

Viktor Frankl, the eminent Viennese psychiatrist, believes that extinguishing human sensitivity by means of 'narcotization' is in a sense a 'spiritual anaesthesia' which can lead to spiritual death. In his opinion (1967, p. 89), 'consistent suppression of intrinsically meaningful emotional impulses because of their possible unpleasurable tone ends in the killing of a person's inner life'. For every emotional experience there is a meaning deeply rooted in human reality. Indiscriminate suppression of unpleasant emotional experiences (such as anxiety) is like the elimination of pain without identifying its underlying cause, and thus a denial of a symptom which conveys a valuable message.

Although the psychoactive drugs are divided here in terms of their primary targets of activity, it is to be noted that their effects on consciousness and mood are not independent. Furthermore, the human organism, with all its diverse neurophysiological systems, functions as a single entity, and it is neither possible nor logical to separate, for instance, the functions of the brain from the other systems. Similarly, there is a unitary basis for human emotions, cognitive and sensorial perceptions and spiritual insight and intuitions. The precise interrelation of the human brain and the soul is far from clear, as the former is matter and can be perceived by our senses, while the latter is not composed of matter and thus is inaccessible to our physical senses for measurement or recognition. The soul is like an energy beyond the grasp of our sensory perception and intellectual determination; yet it continues to prevail in our life, like the power of thought which cannot be touched, seen or measured, but which exists.

The interrelationship of sensory and spiritual powers

Man is endowed with five senses through which he perceives the material world: the powers of sight, hearing, taste, smell and feeling. In addition to these, 'Abdu'l-Bahá, son of the founder of the Bahá'í Faith, describes other dimensions of human reality as follows:

> Man has also spiritual powers: imagination, which conceives things; thought, which reflects upon realities; comprehension, which comprehends realities; memory, which retains whatever man imagines, thinks and comprehends. The intermediary between the five outward powers and the inward powers is the sense which they possess in common – that is to say, the sense which acts between the outer and inner powers, conveys to the inward powers whatever the outer powers discern . . . For instance, sight is one of the outer powers; it sees and perceives this flower, and conveys this perception to the inner power – the common faculty – which transmits this perception to the power of imagination, which in its turn conceives and forms this image and transmits it to the power of thought; the power of thought reflects and, having grasped the reality, conveys it to the power of comprehension; the comprehension, when it has comprehended it, delivers the image of the object perceived to the memory, and the memory keeps it in its repository. (*Some Answered Questions*, pp. 210–11)

From this explanation we can appreciate the chain by which messages from the outer world of matter are carried to the inner world of reality. These messages may excite or inhibit emotion, resulting in the alteration of mood and feeling. They may spark intellectual activity and bring about a new thought or idea. It is important to note, however, that under certain conditions the perception of the sensory organs and the interpretation of the perceived images or messages may become distorted, thus giving rise to an incorrect impression of an external reality.

As an example, in a state of alcoholic delirium a rose may be perceived not as a rose, but rather as a frightening object creeping into the observer's mind and arousing tremendous fear and anxiety. The consumption of an intoxicant causes a misperception of reality which in this case is defined as an illusion. Psychedelic substances such as LSD and mescaline may alter the perception and interpretation of messages received by the brain from the outer powers or external stimuli. As a result, visual and auditory experiences may be perceived in a highly exaggerated manner or may be interpreted illogically and irrationally. Substances can also affect the inner powers, particularly the power of imagination and the grasp of reality, with resulting impairment of judgement and false perceptual experiences.

The human mind, as described by 'Abdu'l-Bahá, is the power of the human spirit or the rational soul.

> Spirit is the lamp; mind is the light which shines from the lamp. Spirit is the tree, and the mind is the fruit. Mind is the perfection of the spirit, and is its essential quality, as the sun's rays are the essential necessity of the sun. (ibid. p. 209)

Through this image from the Bahá'í writings, where the soul is likened to the tree and the mind to the fruit of the tree, it is possible to consider the mental faculties such as intelligence, imagination, memory, reason, comprehension and the power of discovery which are collectively referred to as the mind, as the fruits of the soul (Figure 4). The natural strength of all these intellectual faculties can be altered by chemical substances. Should these substances be used without medical consultation to ensure their proper indication and safety, the adverse effects resulting from their misuse may ultimately affect the evolution of the soul and the development of its powers through the human mind and character.

Figure 4
The rational soul and its attributes

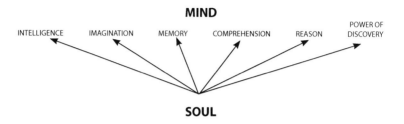

In the Bahá'í concept of the reality of man (Bahá'u'lláh and 'Abdu'l-Bahá, *The Reality of Man*, p. 9), the soul occupies a unique place in the life of an individual. It is a centre for human reality around which revolve the intellectual, emotional, physical, social and cultural dimensions of human existence. These various dimensions or forces are not isolated from each other, but rather flow into one another (Figure 5). In a well-balanced life, the soul remains as the centre of spiritual gravity bringing all other essential forces into creative harmony and interaction. Some individuals, because of their innate potential and perception and aided by education, may make more significant progress in one of these aspects of life than in others. For example, among those who excel in the intellectual sphere, we find the great scholars of the arts and sciences, while others who are enlightened and advanced spiritually and morally are those we intuitively recognize as 'saints'. There are yet others who have made special progress in physical development, such as athletes or dancers. It is to be noted, however, that progress in any one facet of human development may or may not be associated with changes in other dimensions. A learned scholar may attain significant insight into the mystery of the universe, or become a media celebrity, or drift into a reclusive life. Man possesses tremendous potential for growth and progress, the fulfilment of which depends, among other things, on his freedom from excessive material attachments which will distort his perception of his true self. He should therefore safeguard the energies with which he is endowed by adhering to a healthy standard of life. It is indi-

Figure 5
The multidimensional nature of the human being

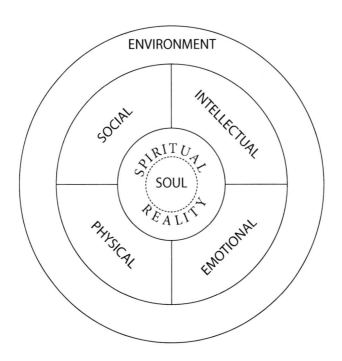

cated in the Bahá'í writings that:

> These energies with which . . . [God] hath endowed the reality of
> man lie, however, latent within him, even as the flame is hidden
> within the candle and the rays of light are potentially present in the
> lamp. The radiance of these energies may be obscured by worldly
> desires even as the light of the sun can be concealed beneath the
> dust and dross which cover the mirror . . . unless the dross is
> blotted out from the face of the mirror it can never represent
> the image of the sun nor reflect its light and glory. (Bahá'u'lláh,
> *Gleanings*, pp. 65–6)

10

SPIRITUAL DIMENSIONS OF SUBSTANCE ABUSE PREVENTION

Reflection on Life and its Purpose

Human life on this planet is like the life of a traveller. In any journey there is a search, a purpose and a destiny. The purpose of the journey gives meaning to the traveller's effort and the destiny becomes the ultimate point of fulfilment of that purpose. The guiding light of any journey is the power of intellect and the capacity to discern the right path and be committed to persevering and reaching the destination. The power of intellect itself is an expression of the rational soul, which transcends any material limitation. In another analogy, the human brain may be likened to a mirror and the spirit to the sun. In order for the sun to manifest its power, the mirror needs to be well positioned and clear of any dust or dross that may obscure or prevent the light of the sun from being reflected in it. Illicit drugs are like the dust that will obscure and darken the mirror of the intellect.

Given the above metaphors, we can appreciate how the adverse effects of drugs on the mind can affect human perception and behaviour in such a way that the true purpose and meaning of life will be lost and its goal become nothing but an illusion. A spiritual perspective on life and its ultimate destiny gives a different meaning to life. It defines not only our relationship to ourselves, but also our relationship with our future beyond this world, with the universe and its Creator. In the light of this concept, mind- and mood-altering drugs of an illicit nature become products of manipulation of the power of intellect to obtain satisfaction and to perpetuate pleasure in an artificial way. Research studies show that when the pleasure centre of the brain is frequently stimulated by substances such as cocaine, dopamine activities will steadily increase. The pleasure centre then becomes dependent on that substance in order to maintain a pleasurable feeling. The result is the addiction of some brain cells to the external substance – cocaine, morphine, heroin, and so on.

The purpose of religious teachings is to protect the human mind and soul, and to educate the masses so that they can adopt sound and healthy lifestyles that will contribute to the well-being of society and the progress of civilization. Research studies (Pardini et al. 2000) show that religious faith and spirituality are associated with more positive mental and physical health outcomes. More specifically, religious involvement has been found to be associated with fewer high risk behaviours such as alcohol abuse (Koenig et al, 1994). Some aspects of religious faith have been linked to positive mental health outcomes such as lower levels of depression and suicide and higher levels of self-esteem (Pardini, p. 347). In their research study of 236 persons recovering from a substance abuse problem, Pardini et al, (2000, p. 351) reported that most individuals recovering from substance abuse had some type of religious affiliation with a high level of religious faith. One of the reasons for this positive effect is that religious teachings educate people about spiritual attitudes, toward themselves as well as toward others, and also toward the environment and the Creator.

If we ponder a simple day-to-day challenge such as drinking alcohol, we note that millions of people suffering from physical and mental disorders caused by the consumption of alcohol could have been saved had they abstained from it. As we have seen (Chapter 2 in this book), in the United States 15.4 million adults are victims of alcoholism. With this number come an additional 56 million people who are affected by the alcohol abuse or addiction of the former group. In other words, 70 million Americans are affected by direct or indirect consequences of alcohol consumption (APA 1994). In Russia the toll of alcohol consumption and its tragic consequences is even higher. Religious principles prohibiting the consumption of alcohol no doubt would have implications for the lives of these and millions more people worldwide.

Given that alcoholic disability can be transmitted to the foetus and affect the newborn infant, thousands upon thousands of children with foetal alcohol syndrome (FAS) could have been spared this life-long and preventable affliction. The American Psychiatric Association reported (1994, p. 5) that over 8,000 American babies are born each year with FAS. This human tragedy, which results from choice of lifestyle and indulgence in pleasure-seeking behaviour such as consumption of alcohol or illicit drugs is preventable: 'what can be started can also be stopped', as the Queen of Sweden said in her talk to the UN General Assembly in 1998 (see box on pp. 34–35 above). If we add the social, emotional, economic and other losses to the list of physical complications of substance abuse, we may realize the enormity of this self-induced calamity of our time which has affected all nations of the world.

The teachings of the Bahá'í Faith, which encourage harmony between scientific facts and religious values, draw attention to the fact that we need to be not only spiritual but also sensible in our attitude toward any tampering with our mind – our reality – which may lead to our abasement and destruction.

According to the teachings of Bahá'u'lláh a human being is a 'supreme Talisman', 'a mine rich in gems of inestimable value' (Bahá'u'lláh, *Gleanings*, pp. 259–60). The purpose of life in this world is to fulfil the potential with which each individual is endowed, and collectively to build a just and ever-advancing civilization through service to humanity. Enlightened and proper education is the key to uncovering the 'gems' of human reality. But the life experiences we choose can impede or enhance that educational process. The illicit use of alcohol and drugs is an impediment to the realization of noble potentials.

The Bahá'í Faith regards human thought and intellect, rather than the physical frame, as one's reality ('Abdu'l-Bahá, *Paris Talks*,

p. 4). Indeed, human intellect has been exalted as 'the most precious gift bestowed upon man by the Divine Bounty' (ibid. p. 41). Ironically, it is the intellect, that 'most precious gift', which is targeted by the intoxicating effects of substances of abuse as an exchange for pleasure! In a world so advanced and sophisticated, with scientific discoveries and new medications to alleviate pain and suffering, why is it that on the one hand physicians strive to heal a mind afflicted with schizophrenia, and that on the other hand millions of young people willingly submit their mind and intellect to the nefarious effects of illicit drugs, some of which (i.e. cocaine) can cause mental disorders with symptoms not very different from those of schizophrenia or other psychotic states?

Harmonizing the Scientific and Religious Viewpoints

What is missing in our science, our logic or our society, that we are willing to take such a serious risk for temporary satisfaction? Is religion or religiosity an answer? Critics disagree, arguing that some of these drugs, particularly cannabis and hashish, were used in religious ceremonies and rituals in order to attain 'spiritual' ecstasy and inspiration (such as the use of cannabis by pre-Christian Hindus and also hashish by followers of a Muslim sect in the past). The fact is, none of these practices were prescribed by the religions at the source of revelation. It was their followers, mostly belonging to certain sects or offshoots of the religion, who created such rituals. True religious teachings have been against the consumption of mind-altering drugs in the name of spiritual realization. Accordingly, there is a need to harmonize religious belief with proven scientific facts and logic in the service of the human mind and soul.

These emphatic words of a divine Manifestation are a call to humanity to recognize its richness and nobility in creation:

O Son of Spirit!
I created thee rich, why dost thou bring thyself down to poverty?
Noble I made thee, wherewith dost thou abase thyself? Out of the essence of knowledge I gave thee being, why seekest thou

enlightenment from anyone beside Me? Out of the clay of love I moulded thee, how dost thou busy thyself with another? Turn thy sight unto thyself, that thou mayest find Me standing within thee, mighty, powerful and self-subsisting. (Bahá'u'lláh, *Hidden Words*, Arabic 13)

Drug abuse or a search for identity?

One explanation for the decline of humanity from its inner wealth and nobility to poverty and abasement through alcohol and intoxicants is that people are searching for their true identity, the meaning of life. In other words, in a social analysis of substance abuse, we may realize that this is a chemical search for truth about life and its destiny. Not all drug users are pleasure addicts; some are searching to find themselves, alas to their detriment. If we were to reflect on the divine source of our creation, perhaps we would not engage in this chemical search for our true self. Bahá'u'lláh reminds us in these words: 'Thou are My lamp and My light is in thee. Get thou from it thy radiance and seek none other than Me' (*Hidden Words*, Arabic 11). Can we say that many of us become too attached to the lamp without recognizing the light within it? Are we too preoccupied with our bodies – have we lost contact with our souls?

The answer to this question requires a faith, a system of belief to which alienated youth and a discouraged humanity can turn for guidance, direction and fulfilment. When such a faith and spiritual belief are absent in a world engulfed in life crises that bring anguish and helplessness, psychoactive drugs become an attractive option at the moment of despair.

Having faith and a sense of connection to a heavenly power may not immediately dispel sorrow or solve social injustice, but they offer a hope and meaning to life which alcohol or narcotics are unable to give. Human beings are highly resilient to life crises if they have faith and social skills, as well as a system of values which enables them to restore their hope in a purposeful and fulfilling life.

The following statement reflects one aspect of such a system

106

of values in the Bahá'í community. It emphasizes refinement of conduct and behaviour:

> Such a chaste and holy life, with its implications of modesty, purity, temperance, decency, and clean-mindedness, involves no less that the exercise of moderation in all that pertains to dress, language, amusements, and all artistic and literary avocations. It demands daily vigilance in the control of one's carnal desires and corrupt inclinations. It calls for the abandonment of a frivolous conduct, with its excessive attachment to trivial and often misdirected pleasures. It requires total abstinence from all alcoholic drinks, from opium, and from similar habit-forming drugs. . . . It can tolerate no compromise with the theories, the standards, the habits, and the excesses of a decadent age. Nay rather it seeks to demonstrate, through the dynamic force of its example, the pernicious character of such theories, the falsity of such standards, the hollowness of such claims, the perversity of such habits, and the sacrilegious character of such excesses. (Shoghi Effendi, *Advent of Divine Justice*, p. 25)

In today's society, personal freedom has been misunderstood:

> Among the highest aspirations of all people is freedom. It is their dream, their expressed ideal, the object of their constant struggle. Yet, few in modern society recognize that purity is the door to freedom, since it is purity that releases a soul from earthly bondage and oppression. (Lample 1999, p. 31)

Anything can be used or abused. But the abuse of mind and intellect can have serious consequences. It can disable the natural powers of the human mind such as perception, memory, judgement and other cognitive functions and capabilities. Substance abuse also influences mood, causing euphoric elation or depression. Many synthetic or natural stimulants (i.e. amphetamines or cocaine) have a direct effect on mood as well as the mind. Without a spiritual understanding of human nature and the purpose of life, and without the assistance of divine knowledge, it is difficult to protect the mind and mood against temptations to experiment with self-induced excitement, however temporary as this may be.

Religious teaching provides a moral framework which contributes to the development of attitudes during childhood. Behavioural attitudes and not mere knowledge shape individual behaviour. They are acquired during early childhood and are adopted later as a way of life. These learned attitudes become values; the values guide judgement about decisions on different behaviours such as to drink or to abstain from drinking.

The notion of 'moderate' drinking

The notion of 'moderate' drinking which is so popular in society at large has been a subject of debate with regard to its validity vis-à-vis the problem of alcoholism. Not only is the term 'moderate' vague and its interpretation variable, but what is 'moderate' for one person may not be so for another. Moreover, it may become very difficult to draw a line between 'moderate' and 'heavy' drinking at times when life stress is severe, one's coping skills are poor and alcohol is available. Many alcoholics were initially 'moderate' drinkers. In view of the complexity of control over drinking, there is a growing idea that complete abstinence from alcoholic beverages presents a much healthier option for prevention. This also applies to other habit-forming and illicit drugs. Alcohol ' . . . is the cause of chronic diseases, weakeneth the nerves and consumeth the mind . . .' ('Abdu'l-Bahá, quoted in Shoghi Effendi, *Advent*, p. 27).

The writings of the Bahá'í Faith are very explicit in their attitude toward the use of these substances. Not only is total abstinence from all alcoholic drinking enjoined, but never before in history has the teaching of a religion been so explicit in describing the effects of toxic substances such as alcohol and narcotics on the human mind and soul.

One of the fundamental principles of the Bahá'í revelation is obedience to its laws. True liberty is to be found in obedience to the ordinances of God. Such obedience in abstaining from toxic substances protects the individual's freedom to be his true self.

The attitude of Bahá'ís around the world towards the consumption of alcohol is based on Bahá'í law as stipulated in the Kitáb-i-Aqdas, Bahá'u'lláh's 'Most Holy Book'. In it the consumption of alcoholic beverages of all kinds and in every form is forbidden. In other writings Bahá'u'lláh explains, 'Become ye intoxicated with the wine of the love of God, and not with that which deadeneth your minds . . .' (ibid. p. 27).

In our present consumer society, it is hard to imagine the existence of a 'wine' that could bring joy and contentment, other than the material kind. But this kind of wine does exist, more powerful than the one that is locked in a cellar. It is the spiritual wine of mystic delight. The spiritual significance of 'mystic wine' is a symbolic expression for the words of the divine Educator. To quaff from the cup of these words causes one to attain spiritual ecstasy. Such spiritual wine, when taken for the good of mankind, excites one's consciousness to achieve a greater understanding of the mysteries of life and the universe, stimulates one's mind and soul to discover a new meaning in life, and broadens one's vision of true love for humanity. None of these attributes can be acquired through the consumption of material wine or other alcoholic and addictive substances. On the contrary, a multitude of scientific observations have demonstrated that alcohol does the opposite, as well as causing confusion, hangovers and withdrawal symptoms.

In praise of the spiritual wine of His Revelation Bahá'u'lláh states:

> O Son of Dust! Turn not away thine eyes from the matchless wine of the immortal Beloved, and open them not to foul and mortal dregs. Take from the hands of the divine Cup-Bearer the chalice of immortal life, that all wisdom may be thine, and that thou mayest hearken unto the mystic voice calling from the realm of the invisible. (Hidden Words, Persian 62)

> Our intention is indeed that wine which intensifieth man's love for God . . . and igniteth in the hearts the fire of God and love for Him, and glorification and praise of Him. So potent is this wine that a drop thereof will attract him who drinketh it to the Court

of His sanctity and nearness, and will enable him to attain the presence of God. (*Compilation*, vol. II, p. 246)

Several letters written on behalf of Shoghi Effendi clarify specific situations for Bahá'ís in their desire to obey the Bahá'í law concerning the use of alcohol. Using liquors containing alcohol for the purpose of adding flavour to food is against Bahá'í principles, as it constitutes a form of consumption (*Lights of Guidance*, p. 351). Nor is it permissible to engage in business enterprises involving the sale or trafficking of alcohol or other illicit drugs (*Compilation*, II, p. 252). Social programmes to promote abstinence from alcohol and non-prescribed drugs, including Alcoholics Anonymous (AA), are encouraged as they contribute to the betterment of humanity (ibid. p. 249).

A spiritual perspective on the non-medical use of drugs

The Bahá'í scriptures are quite emphatic about the prohibition of the non-medical use of opium. 'Abdu'l-Bahá states that opium 'fasteneth on the soul, so that the user's conscience dieth, his mind is blotted away, his perceptions are eroded. It turneth the living into the dead. It quencheth the natural heat' ('Abdu'l-Bahá, *Selections*, p. 149). He goes on to say that the use of opium 'layeth in ruins the very foundation of what it is to be human' (ibid.).

The greatest danger of opium and its derivatives is in the user's rapid development of chemical tolerance, resulting in strong psychological and physiological dependency. Medical research (Ghadirian 1969) indicates that the profound effect of these substances on the cells of the brain and the drug withdrawal symptoms can be serious.

The danger of opium abuse and addiction throughout the world has been a matter of special concern to the United Nations and its Commission on Narcotic Drugs. The Bahá'í International Community, a non-governmental organization (NGO) represented at the United Nations, has cooperated closely with UN agencies in working towards the prevention and eradication of narcotic and other drug abuse.

The attitude of Bahá'ís towards the use of hallucinogens and psychedelic drugs such a mescaline, LSD and cannabis is equally explicit, as shown in the following statements by the Universal House of Justice, the supreme governing body of the Bahá'í Faith:

> Concerning the so-called 'spiritual' virtues of the hallucinogens ... spiritual stimulation should come from turning one's heart to Bahá'u'lláh, and not through physical means such as drugs and agents ... hallucinogenic agents are a form of intoxicant. As the friends, including the youth, are required strictly to abstain from all forms of intoxicants, and are further expected conscientiously to obey the civil law of their country, it is obvious that they should refrain from using these drugs.
>
> A very great responsibility for the future peace and well-being of the world is borne by the youth of today. Let the Bahá'í youth by the power of the Cause they espouse be the shining example for their companions. (Letter, 15 April 1965)

> Bahá'ís should not use hallucinogenic agents, including LSD, peyote, and similar substances, except when prescribed for medical treatment. Neither should they become involved in experiments with such substances. (Letter, 19 May 1966)

When we reflect deeply on the meaning of life we find new concepts of joy and sorrow as they relate to the human soul. Human beings, 'Abdu'l-Bahá explains, are influenced by two sentiments, joy and pain:

> ... all the sorrow and grief that exist come from the world of matter – the spiritual world bestows only the joy!
>
> If we suffer it is the outcome of material things, and all the trials and troubles come from this world of illusion.
>
> For instance, a merchant may lose his trade and depression ensues. A workman is dismissed and starvation stares him in the face. A farmer has a bad harvest, anxiety fills his mind. A man builds a house which is burnt to the ground and he is straightway homeless, ruined, and in despair.

111

All these examples are to show you that the trials which beset our every step, all our sorrow, pain, shame and grief, are born in the world of matter; whereas the spiritual Kingdom never causes sadness. A man living with his thoughts in this Kingdom knows perpetual joy. The ills all flesh is heir to do not pass him by, but they only touch the surface of his life, the depths are calm and serene. ('Abdu'l-Bahá, *Paris Talks*, pp. 110–11)

In our excessive attachment to the material world as a source of comfort and security, joy and pleasure become a form of commodity to acquire through different means, including the consumption of alcohol and stimulants. Such an attachment yields superficial satisfaction but not true joy or lasting fulfilment.

11

AN INTEGRATED APPROACH TO PRIMARY PREVENTION

This book has attempted to increase public awareness of the devastating effects that alcohol and drug abuse have on human lives and achievements. There is an old saying that 'prevention is better than cure'.

Knowledge and attitude in prevention

Primary prevention is aimed at sending a message which will prevent non-drug users from initiating drug consumption. The messages of drug prevention campaigns may be intended to inform, warn, shock or frighten: all these different methods have the purpose of raising individual awareness of the impact of drugs, but not all have a positive effect. For a programme to be effective, it must be culturally appropriate. Success will depend on how well it influences people's knowledge, attitude and behaviour. It is easier to acquire knowledge than to develop new attitudes and behavioural skills. A change of attitude can serve as an indicator of the effectiveness of a prevention programme. Spiritual belief and faith in religious teachings can reinforce human will to overcome drug problems.

Knowledge and attitude are two pillars of an educational

programme for demand reduction and prevention. They are complementary. Knowledge alone has shown to be inadequate in preventive education: it has to be supported by changes in behavioural attitudes.

Components of Prevention

The foremost elements responsible for the expansion of substance abuse include (1) the availability of drugs and (2) the behavioural attitude towards the use of drugs. Reduction or cessation of the availability of illicit drugs is therefore critical to prevention, for production and trafficking of these substances not only makes them more accessible, but also creates an environment conducive to the continuation of their use. The production of synthetic drugs (such as amphetamine derivatives) by clandestine laboratories further complicates control of drug expansion. Government and law-enforcement agencies have concentrated their efforts on intervention in drug trafficking and production, but have so far neglected primary prevention, including systematic and long-term planning for mass education and public-awareness campaigns. Besides these two important elements of drug availability and behavioural attitude, we must recognize that other psychosocial factors play an important role. These are addictive attachment to the substances of abuse, loss of control, and denial: these also need to be addressed in therapy and prevention.

Four types of drug abuse have been identified by the UN International Drug Control Programme (1997):

(a) ritual/cultural;
(b) medical/therapeutic;
(c) social/recreational;
(d) occupational/functional.

Preventive education needs to recognize the cultural as well as the social and occupational parameters of substance abuse problems.

This chapter concentrates mostly on the role of behavioural attitudes and public awareness in primary prevention and their

114

impact on the fall or rise of consumer demand for alcohol or drugs in society. The preventive model suggested is a community-based approach which also recognizes the importance of health promotion. In a primary preventive programme at least three elements can be identified for lines of action (UNODC 1997, pp. 203–206):

- The target population
- The message
- The medium

The target population can be very broad and may embrace the entire population or include specific groups such as children, youth, ethnic minorities, women, older people, and so on.

Information contained in the educational messages should be accurate and objective, free from inflated remarks, exaggeration of the drug consumption risks or shock tactics to create a climate of fear. Otherwise the message may be counterproductive and undermine the credibility of the knowledge conveyed. It may be more effective to concentrate on health promotion and positive profiles of those who abstain from drugs.

In recent years there has been a new trend in substance abuse prevention programmes based on the promotion of a healthy lifestyle. This has involved a shift of focus from 'anti-drug' to 'pro-health'. Emphasis is placed on what makes us healthy, strong and content, as opposed to dwelling on the negative effect of drugs. Schools and other educational establishments are the ideal providers of this kind of large-scale education for prevention. Mass-media campaigns can also have a powerful influence in propagating messages on healthy lifestyle and how to use one's talents and capacities for individual progress.

Stages of prevention

The United National Drug Control Program (UNDCP 1998, pp. 1–3) has identified three stages in preventive education for the reduction of drug consumption:

- *Primary* prevention, which is outlined below and is the focus of this chapter;
- *Secondary* prevention, which identifies individuals in the early stage of experimentation with drugs. Education and counselling are provided to these persons to cease drug use and consider positive and healthier alternatives to drugs; and
- *Tertiary* prevention, which focuses on termination of compulsive drug use by means of treatment and rehabilitation to sustain drug-free behaviour.

Primary Prevention

The goal of primary prevention is to prevent or at least delay the initiation of substance abuse. Public education is the focus of this initial stage of prevention. Information about illicit drugs, and signs and symptoms of their consumption, are provided to the public and particularly to target groups, including those at high risk of substance abuse (ibid.). Primary prevention also promotes healthy lifestyles and a drug-free society by providing positive alternatives to drug abuse and a supportive environment in which there are opportunities to acquire life skills and knowledge about issues ranging from stress management to problem-solving, and to gain a greater existential insight into the purpose of life and beyond.

Any preventive measures taken against problems so pervasive and widespread as drug abuse and alcoholism will have to be comprehensive to be successful and will have to take into consideration all dimensions of human reality. Most existing programmes are aimed at the treatment and rehabilitation of those who are already drug addicts and alcoholics; very few, if any, positive and comprehensive programmes can be found which have been proven to be successful for primary prevention. Instead, governments and private enterprises, directly or indirectly, make significant investments in the production and distribution of alcohol and other habit-forming substances. The media, as well as sports and public events of local, national and international interest, continue to reflect the popular use of alcoholic drinks. It is very rare, at least in the western world, to attend a wedding, anniversary, farewell party or any other celebration where alcoholic beverages are not served. Yet the general consensus is that abuse of alcohol is harmful to human health, and medicine is unable to prevent the heavy toll taken by its effects each year.

Norman Sartorius, former Director of Mental Health at the World Health Organization (WHO), in 1986 pointed out three giant obstacles impeding the task of prevention in the area of drug abuse. The most important of these was, he believed, the low priority given to the maintenance of a healthy lifestyle. Health, here, is defined as 'a harmonious balance . . . between the total environment and oneself . . . in which physical, mental, and social functioning complement each other in maintaining this balance' (Sartorius 1986, pp. 2–3). He felt that pleasure, patriotism, productivity, popularity, esteem of others, physical appearance and attractiveness have all received a higher priority. Twenty years after Sartorius's article, and although there has been some progress in public awareness of the benefits of healthy lifestyles, practice still has not caught up with knowledge. The other two obstacles he mentions are the addictive nature of drugs and today's stressful, and socially and emotionally impoverished environment. For instance, he comments, 'Sharing a cigarette or a drink after a strenuous day may (unfortunately) offer more in human values than anything else available.' Dr Sartorius suggests that prevention lies not only in listing alternative activities or hobbies, or imposing tight restrictions on the production and distribution of drugs, but also in educating people to care about their health and to make mature decisions in order to maintain it (ibid.).

Education does indeed play an important role in prevention, not only through the imparting of information, but also by providing role models for children and adolescents to follow. Unfortunately, many adolescents witness a contradiction in the behaviour and attitudes of their parents and relatives. Early education and parental attitudes play an important role in the formation of the future habits of children. In a family where the mother's daily headache can only be relieved by a sedative or pain-killer; in a home where the father can't sleep without taking a pill and often needs a drink before starting his day; or where a sister has a habit of getting 'stoned' whenever she goes to a party; in a family where the members are over-medicated for their physical aches and pains or their psychological need for security; in all of these circumstances children receive subtle messages which, consciously or subconsciously, contribute to their future attitudes and means of coping with stress. Research on the problems of juvenile alcohol and drug use supports the notion that problem users frequently come from families where one of the parents is alcoholic, or is involved in drug abuse (Information Canada 1972, p. 33).

In order to establish a multidisciplinary and comprehensive plan of prevention a number of elements must be considered. Table 2 on p. 79 showed some of the frequently observed contributing factors in substance abuse, including those of prime importance – the role of the individual, family and culture, childhood education, and the influence of dysphoric moods such as loneliness, depression and personal failure as well as the availability of drugs.

Here is a brief outline of the structural elements of a comprehensive programme for the prevention of adolescent alcoholism and drug abuse. It involves education at three levels: the individual, the family and the society (Figure 6).

Figure 6
Preventive education at three levels: Individual, family and society

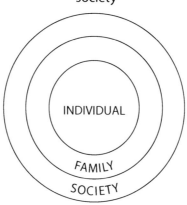

The individual

The individual plays a crucial role in any prevention programme for substance abuse. It is the individual who becomes the first 'consumer' of these products. It is the individual who, by using a bottle of wine or a joint of marijuana, adds to the rise in demand and encourages the production and dissemination of the supply of these substances. It is also the individual who, through his will and action, can contribute significantly to the 'curbing of the epidemic of drug abuse'. Dr C. Stuart Houston (1986) has described the way in which one woman's initiative and perseverance led to an eventual widespread banning of cigarette-smoking in major sectors of the airline and other transportation industries.

Mrs Betty Carnes, of Scottsdale, Arizona was the first to demand and actually obtain a seat in a non-smoking area in an airplane. A frequent commuter from Phoenix to New York City, Mrs Carnes in 1971 persuaded all three airlines flying this route to provide her with a seat in a non-smoking area. Each of the airlines received so many letters of commendation concerning this new practice and so many requests to supply non-smoking sections on their other routes that within a few years most airlines offered seats in non-smoking sections. Regulations were soon introduced to make it compulsory for other airlines. This practice spread to trains and buses and later to many other public places. Mrs Carnes has been recognized by *Business Week* magazine as the individual who started the ball rolling; the spin-off effects are still being felt by the tobacco industry.

That act of courage and determination was a signal victory in raising further public awareness of the adverse effects of cigarette smoking or its passive inhalation. The heavy toll of serious and life-threatening complications of tobacco consumption (such as heart attacks and lung cancer) on the one hand and the efforts of medical and other health professionals to deal with this predicament on the other, made it critical that serious steps be taken to curtail and control cigarette smoking worldwide.

The WHO Framework Convention on Tobacco Control (FCTC) provided the objectives for curbing tobacco consumption in the world. The final FCTC text was adopted unanimously by the World Health Assembly in May 2003. By February 2005 the FCTC entered into force after its ratification by 57 countries. The provisions of the treaty call on countries to:

- Ban all tobacco advertising and promotion within five years of the treaty's entry into force
- Require health warning labels that cover at least 30 per cent of the surface of tobacco packages, within three years
- Protect people from second-hand smoke in all indoor public places and workplaces
- Consider increasing prices and taxes on tobacco products (cited in PAHOtoday, 2005)

A number of countries have adopted comprehensive laws banning the smoking of tobacco at work and in public places, including bars, clubs and restaurants. In March 2004, Ireland became the first country in the world to prohibit smoking in all indoor workplaces including pubs. Norway, New Zealand, Bhutan, and Scotland followed. Legislation has now been passed in seven Australian states, nine Canadian provinces and nine US states banning smoking in certain public and workplaces (Brindley 2006). Other countries too have been promoting a smoke-free environment and legislating the prohibition of smoking in public places, particularly in hospitals, schools, restaurants and other places. In the United Kingdom smoking in public places has been banned since July 2007.

In exploring the role of the individual in prevention, I recommend the following points from the Bahá'í writings for consideration, as increasing personal strength and mindfulness in facing the challenge:

1. *Self-realization.* A human being is distinguished from other species by his spiritual nature. He has been referred to in Bahá'í scripture as 'the supreme Talisman' and has the unique distinction and capacity to know and to love God (Bahá'u'lláh, *Gleanings*, p. 259). Moreover, human beings have been endowed with the gift of understanding, 'God's greatest gift to man' ('Abdu'l-Bahá, *Paris Talks*, p. 32).

120

'Abdu'l-Bahá explains that man possesses two natures, his spiritual or higher nature and his material or lower nature. 'In one he approaches God, in the other he lives for the world alone. Signs of both these natures are to be found in men' (ibid. p. 55). Through his higher nature man expresses positive attributes such as love, mercy, kindness, truth and justice, while through the lower nature he manifests untruth, cruelty, injustice and all which have been referred to as evil. Evil is nothing but the expression of one's lower nature. Noble qualities and good habits are expressions of man's spiritual nature whereas all imperfections and sinful actions are born of the material nature (Figure 7). The ideal self is the one in which the spiritual nature dominates the material nature resulting in the appearance of noble qualities and divine attributes (ibid). The purpose of religion and divine education is to strengthen the higher nature of man and to help him develop basic capacities of

Figure 7
Interrelationship of the higher or spiritual nature and the lower or material nature of man

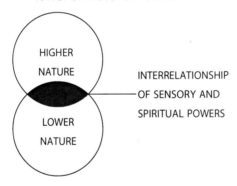

knowing and loving. He should then dedicate these capacities to the service of humanity (Jordan 1968, p. 4). The use of intoxicants and habit-forming drugs will suppress the development of the higher nature while satisfying the desires of the lower nature.

2. *Sense of purpose in life.* Human life should be guided by a sense of purpose which gives meaning to one's existence. According to

Bahá'u'lláh, 'the generating impulse and the primary purpose' of life is to know and to love God (*Gleanings*, p. 65). Such a purpose in life demands a personal effort to acquire divine virtues and noble attributes. These virtues and attributes become qualities of the soul and result in both spiritual and material progress. The Bahá'í teachings expand man's vision to arenas beyond his material self and lower nature. They challenge the individual to invest his energy in the well-being of others. They emphasize that the human spirit during its journey in this world must acquire certain perfections to enlighten it ('Abdu'l-Bahá, *Some Answered Questions*, p. 200). Like a traveller who journeys through cities and countries and becomes acquainted with the cultures and customs of each land and nation, the human spirit, through the experiences of this world, will acquire certain characteristics and virtues as part of its evolution. Life stress, the tests and trials of this world, provide challenges for individual growth and fulfilment. Substances of abuse, however, impede the growth of the individual and offer nothing but illusory pleasure.

3. *Sense of human worth and nobility.* A human being is born noble and should be educated so that he may be able to discover the mystery of his creation and mine the 'gems of inestimable value' which lie within him. Recognition of human nobility in creation is an important step in prevention. It is evident that respect for human worth and dignity should be reinforced as part of a systematic preventive education. We see alcoholics and drug addicts who have lost their self-esteem and their sense of basic human nobility. It is believed, for instance, that the widespread problem of alcoholism among North America's First Nation peoples is partly due to the loss of that sense of dignity and pride in traditional values that they enjoyed prior to the discovery of the American continent by Europeans. In reality, they possess a rich heritage of spiritual traditions and values. The film *Honour of All* (1985) which vividly illustrates a successful rehabilitation programme among them, reflects the struggle of a people devastated by alcoholism to rediscover their true identity and help themselves to regain their dignity and high ideals.

The Baháʼí Faith teaches that the high destiny of each human being in creation should be reflected in his attitude towards himself. Submitting oneself to the destructive effects of alcohol and intoxicating drugs conflicts with one's sense of self-dignity.

Individual commitment to non-drug use is often inspired and maintained by noble values and faith, usually developed during childhood through education, discipline, and the example of parents and the community. Baháʼuʼlláh (here speaking with the voice of the Creator) elucidates the true nature of the self in the following words:

> O My servants! Could ye apprehend with what wonders of My munificence and bounty I have willed to entrust your souls, ye would, of a truth, rid yourselves of attachment to all created things, and would gain a true knowledge of your own selves – a knowledge which is the same as the comprehension of Mine own Being. Ye would find yourselves independent of all else but Me, and would perceive, with your inner and outer eye, and as manifest as the revelation of My effulgent Name, the seas of My loving-kindness and bounty moving within you. (Baháʼuʼlláh, *Gleanings*, pp. 326-7)

4. *True liberty and freedom.* The true meaning of freedom has been largely misunderstood in society. In a permissive society freedom is perceived as the right to do whatever one wishes as long as it does not infringe on the rights of others. In such a society, the individual's rights and responsibilities toward his own self are seriously neglected. When the lower nature takes command, replacing the higher nature, one can say that the person has lost his freedom. Drug dependency will ultimately deprive addicts of their true liberty. The Baháʼí perspective on liberty and freedom is based on obedience to the laws and ordinances of God revealed in each religious dispensation. Such obedience protects one's freedom to be his true self by shielding him from actions which may harm him. Moreover, an individual's degree of maturity may be measured by his ability to postpone immediate gratification of the desires of his lower nature in order to favour

123

the long-term development of his higher nature. The fundamental principle of obedience to Bahá'í laws on the subject of drug abuse provides a framework for the prevention of alcoholism and drug addiction in Bahá'í communities around the world. As we have seen, according to the Bahá'í teachings the consumption of alcohol, narcotic drugs and all other habit-forming substances, unless prescribed for medical treatment, are forbidden and to be strictly avoided.

According to 'Abdu'l-Bahá, freedom comes from the emancipation of self from the captivity of the world of nature. He states (*Selections*, p. 302):

> And among the teachings of Bahá'u'lláh is man's freedom, that through the ideal Power he should be free and emancipated from the captivity of the world of nature; for as long as man is captive to nature he is a ferocious animal, as the struggle for existence is one of the exigencies of the world of nature. This matter of the struggle for existence is the fountain-head of all calamities and is the supreme affliction.

5. *Striving for purity.* Cleanliness and purity are essential virtues for personal and spiritual progress in the journey of this world. To achieve and maintain these attributes one needs to ponder these emphatic words of 'Abdu'l-Bahá (*Bahá'í World Faith*, pp. 335–6):

> O Lord! Give to the people of Bahá cleanliness and holiness in all conditions, purify and free them from all defilement, deliver them from the use of all that is execrated, liberate them from the chains of habits, so that they may be pure and free, clean and spotless, that they may be worthy servants of the Sacred Threshold and may deserve to enter into relation with God. Deliver them from alcohol and tobacco, and save them from opium, the purveyor of madness! Make them companions of the holy breezes, in order that they may know the pleasures of the wine of the love of God, and that they may attain to the joy and the happiness of attraction to the Kingdom of Abhá!

By purity is also meant purity of mind and behaviour and 'freedom from enslavement' of self and passion ('Abdu'l-Bahá, *Selections*, p. 150). It is attaining perfection by exercising self-control and a higher quality of moral character. 'The best of perfections is immaculacy and the freeing of oneself from every defect' (ibid. p. 146).

Chastity is another expression of purity and also reflects the ability to exercise moral control over one's sexual impulses. Sexual desires and needs should be regulated through marriage. The issue of chastity plays an important role in prevention. The soaring increase of transmission of HIV/AIDS through sexual relationships and promiscuity is a testimony to the need to re-examine society's attitude toward self-indulgence and permissiveness in sexual freedom. International efforts to curb the spread of HIV/AIDS transmission through the use of cleaner needles or condoms will not succeed unless there is a radical change of present attitudes and behaviour with regard to sex.

6. *Daring to be different.* Peer pressure in school or in the neighbourhood is a major cause of the spread of drug abuse among youth and is a matter of serious concern. Likewise, at adult social gatherings and parties where alcohol is commonly served, it is a test of will to refrain from drinking and risk being labelled 'different'. Whether one is a youth or an adult, having the courage to be different in an environment where everyone else drinks or uses drugs is a virtue to be commended. While it is easy to join one's peers in the use of alcohol or drugs, the act of exercising one's personal will and individual conviction to resist this temptation is, in itself, a victory. Interestingly, those who dare to be different because of their beliefs very often also win the respect of their colleagues and friends.

Viktor Frankl believes that 'man's main concern is not to gain pleasure or to avoid pain, but rather to see a meaning in life' (1975, p. 179). Substance abuse among youth is, in part, a type of search, a chemical search, to discover a meaning in life. It is a reflection of the crisis felt by those who find no meaning in the social system. Today's youth receive contradictory messages and confusing signals at home and in society. In many parts of the world they are still looked upon as 'older kids' and are not respected or considered to be responsible individuals. So they behave according to these expectations and, as a result, are very often deprived of opportunities to release their full potential to contribute to the advancement of human society.

In recent years a movement led by young people encouraging their peers to 'say no to drugs' and 'yes to life' has begun to grow. Slogans such as 'be smart, don't start' are being heard among children and youth. Youth-to-youth education for prevention can be highly effective and should be an integral part of prevention. The generation gap will be narrowed through a more effective communication with and a better understanding of young people and their potential to contribute to the prevention of substance abuse.

7. *Challenge to serve mankind.* The individual's relationship to his environment is not static; it is dynamic and constantly changing (Jordan 1970). In the Bahá'í Faith each person is challenged to strive for excellence and to fulfil his potential in the journey of this life. Human potential can be unfolded through one's own efforts in the spiritual, psychological, physical and other dimensions of one's reality. Work in the spirit of service is elevated to the rank of worship (Bahá'u'lláh, 'The twelfth Glad-Tidings', in *Tablets*, p. 26). This is unique in the history of social development and it provides an important impetus for personal growth and creativity through a vocation. Furthermore, it releases individual potential for serving mankind in various ways. It presents a healthy and productive answer to the sense of apathy and boredom and the feeling of uselessness so frequently observed in drug-abusing environments (Ghadirian 1991, p. 7). Today, the pervasive problem of drug abuse has penetrated into the workplace. Although drug use on the job may reflect the stress of life and work, it also illustrates the fact that man has not fully recognized that his vocation, in reality, when performed with full sincerity, is service to God as well as to mankind.

8. *Spiritual perspectives.* A spiritual perspective and an awareness of human destiny in this world will assist the individual to

develop a positive attitude toward himself and his future. Such a perception of life, combining faith and reason, will give a new meaning to life which will enable one to relate positively to stressful circumstances. A firm spiritual stance in life enables a person to confidently say 'no' to drugs and alcohol. When we can do this, we discover that true satisfaction, rather than being the result of drug-induced stimulation, comes from within.

9. *Coping with stress.* A certain amount of stress is necessary and useful for human motivation and productivity. But when the degree of stress reaches beyond our ability to respond and adapt, crises will occur. Coping with stress is a process which largely depends upon our perception of it and our ability to respond to it successfully. Two-thirds of visits to family physicians in North America are prompted by stress-related problems. The use of alcohol and drugs can occur as a result of life stress, depression and family or vocational pressure. Some suggestions for coping with stressful life events are as follows (Ghadirian 1987):

(i) To have a clear and sensible understanding of a crisis and its contributing factors. Also to assess one's own personal resources and other available support.

(ii) An individual's perception and attitude towards stress and suffering can determine the outcome of his efforts to cope. Logically, one should acknowledge the reality of the crisis in question and look for a realistic and practical solution. Success in this task depends on personal skill and capability in problem-solving and decision-making. It also depends on emotional tolerance and flexibility in accepting the consequences.

(iii) To evaluate one's personal resources (physical, psychological, social and spiritual) and to regulate professional or social demands accordingly.

(iv) To cooperate rather than compete in goal-oriented activities. The former approaches the Bahá'í ideal of working together in the spirit of unity, while the latter fosters narcissistic self-interest. Moreover, excessive attachment to material success increases the pain of separation from it in times of adversity.

(v) To moderate the load of professional and daily responsibilities according to capability. There is a need for establishing a healthy balance between personal and family life and professional involvement.

(vi) To strengthen individual ties and relationships with friends, relatives and colleagues. If these relationships are intimate and mature, they will serve as a support system in time of crisis. Having someone to love and to share the joy and sorrow of life with is an important factor in dealing with crises. Society should foster the development of positive social bonds to prevent a sense of isolation and loneliness in the community.

(vii) To accept the reality of failure when it is inevitable. To have a personal faith and belief in spiritual truth which gives meaning to life. Reliance on God as the supreme source of power is important.

The family

Because it acts as the foundation of society, the family plays a very important role in the prevention of substance abuse. Parents, especially mothers in the early years, are children's primary examples with respect to their future attitude towards alcohol and drugs. According to a report (Smart 1976, p. 10),

> . . . mother's drinking seems to be more influential than father's and girls are more likely to model parental drinking than boys. Some evidence also suggests that loose control, especially by the mother, and rejection by the father have more effect on drinking and drunkenness than does the actual drinking of parents.

This study further explains the crucial role of the mother as the first educator of children at home. The parental pattern of reacting to the joys or sorrows of life becomes an important model for children. The practice of serving alcohol at home, for example, whatever the reason may be, can influence children's attitude towards its consumption. Therefore, the parents can provide a healthy and 'drug'-free environment for their children through their abstinence from drugs and alcohol.

It is in the home and family environment that the cornerstone of internal control over one's instincts and desires is laid. If this control is not established at the proper time, an external control may need to be imposed through social rules and regulations. If neither internal nor external controls are developed, a sense of permissiveness prevails in society, which, together with the easy availability of drugs, results in a rise in the level of drug addiction.

Children and adolescents are the most vulnerable targets for drugs of all kinds.

> The growing child is in search of love, understanding and emotional support. But when these are not forthcoming, drugs may become the supporting crutch. Unfortunately, these are crutches that cripple! . . . In cities of both the industrialized and developing world, children are turning to drugs as a result of such deficiencies, lack of proper playgrounds and recreation facilities, lack of programmes to develop social and creative skills, and lack of a home and social environment providing sufficiently for such needs as affection, understanding, encouragement, support, friendship and a feeling of personal worth (Ling and Boutle 1979, pp. 10, 13).

In the Bahá'í view, educating children about the relationship of a person to his/her Creator and to himself/herself is of the utmost importance. The former strengthens their faith and their obedience to the laws and precepts of religion, while the latter helps them to understand that they are entrusted with the precious gift of life. In an analogy, the human body is likened to a temple from which the light of divine reality shines forth. Each person is responsible for the well-being of his own 'temple' and the light of spirit within it. Children thus need to be taught to recognize the nobility of their natures and the creative purpose of their lives.

Childhood education should also emphasize the necessity of accepting hardship, discomfort and adversity as essential components of growth and maturity. Children must acquire the capacity to postpone the instant gratification of their desires and develop a degree of tolerance and maturity. Adolescents have the dual task of adjusting to their internal psycho-biological changes and coping, like adults, with the stresses of a rapidly changing world around them. In this psychosocial climate of change and transition, they may find the task of adaptation distressing, particularly if adults are not sensitive to their needs. In their search for solutions to their problems they may turn to psychoactive drugs. Parents need to understand this in their children and help them recognize the nature of their psychological rhythms and impulses. The youth should also be made aware of an awakening spiritual drive leading them on a search for their true identity. Parents and society bear the crucial responsibility of providing the young with tasks that will translate their motivation, zeal and idealism into productive service to humanity, and will encourage them to discover for themselves the wealth of noble attributes with which they are endowed and which can be reflected in their lives.

Communication is another important issue in the prevention or treatment of adolescent alcohol and drug problems. Harsh and humiliating reactions on the part of parents or other adults to the discovery that a child is using drugs may only lead to further feelings of tension, isolation, and alienation. Instead, if the parents are able to communicate with tact and understanding in a non-threatening manner, they may learn important facts about why their child has become involved with drugs. If parents approach this issue with sincerity and loving care, the adolescent may respond with greater trust, allowing a new level of communication and understanding to develop.

Adolescents need strong role models at home and in society. Many of them, particularly those who come from broken homes, are deprived of the opportunity to identify with such a model. A sense of mistrust towards parents can make it extremely difficult for some children to identify with their parents and to communicate their feelings and frustrations to them. In this case they may turn to their peers, with whom they can share their feelings without fear or embarrassment, to the total exclusion of their parents.

Andrew Mecca, a researcher in the field of drug use, believes that 'establishing a sense of identity and purpose, believing in one's personal worth and ability to meet the challenge of a modern life, and gaining a clear idea of what successful living might mean are all conditions that help young people resist the temptation of drug abuse' (1978, p. 144). Children who have a more positive view of themselves and possess greater self-confidence are more likely to be able to face the stresses of life without resorting to drugs. Mecca concludes that the existing system tends to encourage negative values and reinforce problems rather than to enhance the positive aspects of life.

The Canadian Commission of Inquiry into the Non-Medical Use of Drugs, after extensive review of the literature and with reference to the work of R.H. Blum and his associates, proposed the following list of risk factors to help identify those families whose children are more likely to use drugs (Information Canada 1973, pp. 26–7). The Commission divided the families into those with high risk and those with low risk. The high-risk families, that is to say, those in which the children have higher chances of becoming drug users, are characterized by:

1. Parents who are uncertain of their role as parents and marital partners;
2. A mother who tends to be dominant and a father who lacks leadership in the family;
3. Permissiveness on the part of parents who are either insecure about their own values or are hesitant to implant certain values in their children;
4. A loss of the balance between affection and discipline in the child-rearing process;
5. Discomfort within the family in expressing emotional feeling – family members tending to resort to intellectualization instead;
6. A relationship between husband and wife which does not generate a sense of security and confidence among the children;
7. Poor communication between the parents and the children;
8. Fairly heavy reliance on various drugs on the part of parents;
9. A lack of religious belief, and hostility towards authority.

The low-risk families are described as follows: families who, by contrast with the former group, exhibit a very strong, warm, well-integrated pattern of family life, with a good combination of affection and discipline; there are warm and happy relations between the parents who accept the role as parents and as husband and wife, with leadership from the father that is authoritative but not autocratic – gentle, but firm, and tempered with humour; the parents are confident that they know how to bring up their children and are clear as to the values which they want to transmit, with emphasis on faith in God, respect for parents, self control, tolerance and respect for one another. Within this framework of standards and discipline, children are in fact given considerable scope for freedom and personal responsibility.

Because they know what the parents expect, they appear to be much more confident in their judgments. The children of low-risk families are found to be resistant to peer group pressure. Because of the direction and support they receive in the family, they do not seem to be as dependent on the approval or guidance of others. It is noteworthy that the parents and children of low-risk families are much more forgiving of themselves and each other. They like themselves and each other. They do not expect too much of each other (ibid.).

Although leadership in the family is ascribed to the father in the above outline of the Commission, the mother's role is equally important and cannot be over-emphasized.

The Commission also noted that it is very important for parents to express their ideals through action rather than words. For example, if the parents themselves make use of drugs and alcohol, the reasons they give against the use of these substances will not be convincing to their children. They have already set by their actions an example which their words cannot change.

Family unity and the solidarity of the marital relationship also play an important role in prevention. Experience shows that separation and divorce, and other kinds of marital breakdown, are responsible for a large number of substance abuse cases, particularly alcohol dependencies. An example of this was illustrated in the research work of the present author cited in an earlier chapter, where it was found that a substantial number of student substance abusers came from families where parents were separated or divorced.

Society

Drug abuse is primarily a health issue. Society bears an important responsibility in the area of prevention of substance abuse. Any prevention programme should be aimed at educating all strata of human society at the grass-roots level. Such a programme will involve local communities, sports and cultural centres, schools, child-guidance services, health professionals, counsellors, educators, entertainers and law-enforcement agencies. Society should draw upon its resources for enforcing rules pertaining to the control of illicit drug *supply* and its *trafficking,* and restriction of *demand* – limiting it to those in need of medical treatment.

Given a coherent system of education, individuals can recognize the dual character of drugs: drugs can heal when used properly under the guidance of the medical profession or destroy when self-administered. In view of the fact that a large number of analgesic and psychotropic drugs are habit-forming, and because in many countries some of these drugs are available over the counter and without prescription, it is essential to educate people about the dangers of self-medication. It is estimated that approximately 70 per cent of all cases of drug dependence and abuse result from the misuse of drugs such as sedatives and tranquillizers (WHO 1987). This figure reveals the formidable challenge that the medical profession needs to meet in a global programme for the prevention of drug abuse. Unfortunately the drive for instant satisfaction and the desire for immediate relief from pain and discomfort are so strong in contemporary industrial societies that accomplishment of this task will not be easy.

As the workplace is one of the environments in society where consumption of tobacco, alcohol and illicit drugs can become harmful to the health and safety, preventive rules and educational programmes need to be adopted. One example of this is the ILO

(International Labour Organization) Code of Practice, 1996 which emphasizes the preventive approach. This code:

- calls for joint assessment by employers and workers and their representatives of the effects of alcohol and drug use on the workplace and their cooperation in developing a written policy for the enterprise;
- defines alcohol and drug-related problems as health problems and establishes the need to deal with them, without any discrimination, like any other health problem at work;
- recommends that workplace drug and alcohol policies should cover all aspects of the prevention, reduction and management of alcohol- and drug-related problems and that the relevant information, education and training programmes be integrated, where feasible, into broad-based human resources development, working conditions or occupational safety and health programmes; and
- goes a long way towards establishing the ethical principles vital to concerted and effective action, such as the confidentiality of personal information and the authority of the employer to discipline workers for employment-related misconduct, even where it is associated with the use of alcohol and drugs. (ILO 2006, p. 36)

Health professionals need to educate the public with regard to placing greater value on health. The concept of health should include all dimensions: physical, psychological, social, and spiritual. Through conferences, workshops and seminars, the public should be educated in the *rational* use of prescribed and over-the-counter medications. Health professionals who dedicate their time, knowledge and skills to the treatment of patients, including drug addicts and alcoholics, also need to demonstrate through their actions the importance of abstinence from these substances. Abstinence from alcohol, a substance that is so pervasive in today's society, will be a serious moral challenge to physicians and other health professionals who know well the harmful effects of it on the mind and body. Auguste Forel, a well-known Swiss physician and professor who was director of a psychiatric hospital in the area of Zurich, was particularly impressed by the success of a shoemaker in treating alcoholic patients. While Forel used to refer some of his alcoholics to this shoemaker, he was embarrassed to admit that a simple shoemaker was more successful than he was in the treatment of alcoholism. One day Forel asked the shoemaker about the mystery of his success.

> 'I want you to explain something,' [said Forel]. 'I am a psychiatrist, employed as director of the asylum to heal the sick, and you are a shoemaker; how is it, then, that I have never yet been able to cure a drunkard permanently, while you are so successful?' To this the shoemaker replied with an understanding smile: 'It's very simple, Herr Direktor: I'm an abstainer, and you are not!' 'Yes,' I said, 'I've really felt that for a long while and I've secretly felt ashamed that I've never yet had the courage to begin . . . But now there must be an end of all that. Here is my hand on it; from this day forward I am an abstainer!' (Forel 1937, pp. 159–60)

This experience had a decisive influence on Forel's career and his attitude towards drinking. On that very day he and his wife pledged to abstain from alcohol. He became an energetic promoter of abstinence and was one of the most active members of the International Organization of Good Templars (ibid. p. 326).

Population at risk

Although everyone is potentially at risk for drug and alcohol dependence, certain segments of society are particularly vulnerable, if they are not adequately informed of the hazards of alcohol and drug use and provided with practical alternatives. These are the young, the elderly, patients with chronic pain who depend largely on analgesics and sedatives, and those who suffer from emotional instability and seek the calming effect of tranquillizers, sedatives or alcoholic drinks. Professionals in various fields, including medicine, who are expected to perform with high levels of efficiency and are exposed to continuous demands, may be unable to cope with the stress involved and may consequently turn to alcohol or sedatives for relief. Minorities and individuals suffering from any abrupt and serious material or affectional deprivation as a result of war or social injustice may present a potential risk for substance abuse. In recent years the number of women and schoolchildren involved in substance abuse has increased alarmingly and this phenomenon presents a new challenge for prevention to parents and health educators.

As we have seen in Chapter 5, more and more women are drinking alcohol and smoking cigarettes in the western world. The rise of alcoholic women is particularly alarming. Today women have the difficult task of fulfilling their responsibilities as wives, mothers and career women in society. In a world where the equality of men and women is long overdue, women are still struggling to find their place in diverse socio-economic realms of human society. This is bound to cause an enormous amount of pressure and stress, particularly in countries where women still are deprived of their rights. Loneliness is one of the most common contributing factors to alcoholism among women and has important implications for prevention programmes.

The following case reported by author Brigid McConville in her book *Women Under the Influence* (1983) illustrates the dilemma of many western women:

> My neighbors used to say to me, 'Jane, *why* do you drink? You've got four lovely children, a good home, a good husband.' I used to blame my husband and all sorts of things, but I really didn't know why I drank. Once I started I just couldn't stop.
>
> It was my youngest son, Malcolm, who was most affected by my drinking. He was withdrawn and didn't play with other kids. He went to a special school three days a week and he asked to be called Malcolm at one school, and Nigel, his second name, at the other. I didn't believe it was anything to do with my drinking. I rationalised that it was his teacher's fault, or that he was like his father, a loner.
>
> I was ashamed of myself, and full of guilt about the effect on my family and about not being a 'normal' mother. I always

wanted to be a 'good' mother – one who baked and sewed and sang lullabies and kept a beautiful home. But none of those things came naturally to me . . .

I married at nineteen and had a child in my first year. I started taking amphetamines for depression. They made me feel good and beautiful, and I thought then that I could match up to my sister-in-law's standards. I remember sitting there sewing for hours.

At twenty-five I was sent to a mental hospital because of my addiction to amphetamines. When I came out I started to go to pubs to drink 'socially' with friends. Booze made me feel good, the same as pills had, and beautiful.

But I drank more than my friends. I always wanted more, drank faster and I wanted to stay until the bell rang in the pub. I could never stop . . . After about three years of drinking at home I had no relationship with my family whatsoever. My daughter told me only last week that the children thought the lady who drank came out of a bottle; it wasn't their mum. But I didn't know this . . . Then my eldest daughter left home, and the twins were teenagers and always staying out. Just little Malcolm was there and going to the pub for my booze. I made him come home from school to get my bottle at lunchtime. I stayed in my bedroom mostly. I was dirty. I didn't wash or cook.

I used to wander sometimes in the streets. At forty I went to the Embankment to try and be a hippy. I went to a disco that my daughter went to. I made obscene phone calls. I kept running away. My home life was just a mess. I was desperately lonely and afraid.

Then a lady I knew came to talk to me. She didn't condemn me or ask me *why* I was drinking. She just asked if I had a problem. It was a tremendous relief to be able to say yes. She spoke to me with love and understanding. She came with me to a phone box and I phoned AA (Alcoholics Anonymous). That was six years ago . . . Two years ago my two sons were killed in accidents, little Malcolm six weeks after his elder brother. Without the fellowship of AA I would never have survived it . . . People who are not alcoholic sometimes drink for the same reasons I did – because they feel inadequate or tired. But they don't go on drinking. In the alcoholic, the feelings of guilt, fear and anger go *so* deep . . . My anger leaves me physically and mentally exhausted even now.

So many women don't have a feeling of self-worth. There is so much pressure on us to be thin, to be glamorous, to be the career girl, to be happy with house and kids. Yet some of the happiest people I know are just everyday ordinary people, (pp. 5–10)

Another population group at special risk of abusing certain drugs, and particularly alcohol, is the offspring of parents who were alcoholics. Genetic predisposition among these individuals has made them particularly vulnerable to this disease.

Entertainers and celebrities are exceptionally prone to the influence of alcohol and drug dependency. This is so not only because of the prevailing atmosphere of permissiveness and easy accessibility to drugs in the entertainment field, but also because of the fact that their vocational environment, especially in entertainment, demands an emotional excitement which they may not always be able to deliver to their audience without stimulation.

Special attention should be paid to substance abuse among the elderly, whose number is rising in society. Alcohol is the foremost substance of abuse among this population group. They, too suffer from loneliness and often resort to alcohol in order to forget the harsh reality of their lives. To many of the deprived and lonely elderly, alcohol is the only source of pleasure. Many of these individuals have lost their spouses or close relatives and friends, and their children have established their own independent lives. The term 'empty nest syndrome' reflects the loneliness of the elderly who miss the warmth and joy of having their dear ones with them. It was reported (Dobbie 1977) that between 1969 and 1973 the death rate for women over 60 years of age who suffered from the toxic effects of alcohol rose 500 per cent in Canada. During the same period the death rate from consumption of alcohol combined with other drugs in the same population increased by 67 per cent. Besides alcohol, the misuse or abuse of prescribed drugs and medications obtained over the counter is frequently observed among the older population. Denial is quite common among these people, who fear that to admit their problem may cause them to be deprived of their only source of satisfaction in a lonely and unfriendly world.

Alternatives to drug abuse

Active participation by individual members of a community in a programme based on mutual cooperation and unity of purpose can promote healthy growth within the community. In an ideal environment, youth are continuously encouraged and challenged to participate in various programmes and activities. 'Unless our social system', declares Saul Levine, a psychiatrist, 'can instil in its youth some degree of purpose and community, then in a substantial number of our adolescents problems will inevitably occur' (Levine 1980, p. 33).

There are many ways in which children and adolescents, through the efforts of family and society, can be helped to recognize their full potential and value as human beings. The following activities are suggested as some possible means of encouraging the development of the whole person through the development of intellectual, physical, emotional, social and spiritual capacities, and could form part of a comprehensive programme to prevent substance abuse:

1. *Intellectual activities.* As Allan Cohen pointed out (1971), these provide sensory, perceptual and intellectual stimulation of a creative nature, e.g. essay contests in literature, science or history, or learning about art, music or philosophy. They encourage involvement in the acquisition of new knowledge and provide ideas to help overcome mental apathy and boredom.

2. *Physical activities.* These encourage physical, vocational and creative development and hence increase well-being and self-esteem through the acquisition and perfection of new skills. Youth can also be motivated towards a greater involvement with nature through appreciation of its beauty and by responding to its challenge through various outdoor activities, e.g. outdoor work, gardening, sports, exercise, adventure and survival challenges, and so on (ibid.).

3. *Emotional expression and communication.* These cultivate a spirit of love and fellowship among youth and encourage a greater tolerance for distress and discomfort. They also help to facilitate communication and the expression of feelings of joy, sadness, or anger, and to prevent a sense of isolation. As an example, art, drama and music can help many under-assertive people to express their feelings in a meaningful way.

4. *Social activities and support systems.* These aim at developing a model of education, universal in scope, which would provide equal opportunities for everyone to serve and to be useful to humanity, as well as cultivating a sense of determination, hope and enthusiasm for the realization of high ideals such as the peace and unity of mankind. They enable youth to become involved in humanitarian activities such as serving the underprivileged and disabled, and are a positive force in counteracting the self-centeredness and boredom of modern life. It has been suggested that 'excessive drug use often reflects an excessive preoccupation with self – with one's needs, state of mind, sensations, discomforts and pleasures – and an insufficient involvement with others. Involvement in being of service to others can act as a prevention and a remedy' (Information Canada 1973, pp. 237–8).

Alcoholics Anonymous (AA), one of the largest and most successful organizations in the world for the rehabilitation and prevention of alcoholism, founded its basic philosophy of faith, commitment and the helping relationship on broad spiritual values. The primary objective of AA is to help its members to stay sober and to help other alcoholics achieve sobriety. One of its basic precepts is to help others as a means to one's own rehabilitation (ibid.). In a similar vein, in the Bahá'í writings the highest expression of personality is seen as service to society, a concept that encourages a helping attitude toward all humanity.

In the principles and practice of AA we find the well-known Twelve Steps that illustrate the fundamental character of this successful international organization. Some of the Steps correspond closely to the Bahá'í concepts of the spiritual relationship between the individual and his Creator. For example, one Step speaks of the presence of 'a Power greater than ourselves' to maintain our health. Another Step says '[we] made a decision to turn our will and our lives over to the care of God as we understand Him'.

AA also has Twelve Traditions which are implemented in their group meetings and in support of one another. Here again we find certain principles which are essentially spiritual and play an important role in the preventive processes and rehabilitation. An example from these Twelve Traditions is the statement, 'For our group purpose there is but one ultimate authority – a loving God as He may express Himself in our group conscience. Our leaders are but trusted servants; they do not govern.' This point corresponds very closely to the Bahá'í concept of servitude as the highest expression of personal growth. The Twelve Traditions of AA emphasize the importance of unity for personal recovery and the fact that the only requirement for AA membership is a desire to stop drinking. They also emphasize the importance of putting principles before personalities. The strength of this system is in reliance on God and on a helping relationship in the spirit of honesty, integrity and sincerity.

One of the most touching prayers recited by the members of AA is the following:

> God grant me the serenity to accept the things I cannot change, courage to change the things I can, and wisdom to know the difference.

Another role for society in the area of prevention is the crucial one of increasing public awareness of the growing danger of drug problems, through the educational system. All elementary and high schools should include in their curriculum a clear, objective presentation of the nature and adverse effects of alcohol and substances of abuse. I believe it is as important to know these facts of life as it is to gain knowledge of traditional school subjects such as science, art, history or physical education. There should be a greater emphasis in the educational system on the subject of health and the true purpose of life and its meaning. Unfortunately, the current curriculum of schools is narrowly structured toward the accumulation of information; very little attention is given to the unfolding of human capacity or its inner potential.

Society needs to help adolescents to channel their potential into useful and fulfilling activities and provide ample opportunities for intellectual, emotional and spiritual stimulation, thus eliminating the desire for alcohol and drug-induced excitement.

Other considerations: The availability of drugs

The availability of substances of abuse is another important factor in prevention. It has been known for over a quarter of a century (Domestic Council Drug Abuse Task Force 1975) that there is a direct relationship between the reduction of drug supply and the decline of consumer demand for drugs. While the former is the task of the government and law-enforcement agencies, the latter is a sacred educational duty of individuals, families and society at large.

An example of the influence of drug availability on the spread of drug use is the Japanese experience. Immediately after World War II, amphetamines became readily available in Japan and an epidemic of amphetamine use swept a nation which, except for this incident, was known to have low rates of alcohol and drug use. In the United States, the passage of the Harrison Act in 1914 made opiates illegal for the first time; following this the number of opiate users dropped to half of what it had been previously (ibid.).

Gabriel Nahas of Columbia University, in his article 'Prevention: The only solution' (1987), extends this issue further by indicating how the availability and acceptability of drugs played a decisive role in the spread of drug addiction in history:

> Records of history show that in societies where dependence-producing drugs are socially acceptable and easily available, they are widely consumed, and their usage is associated with a high incidence of individual and social damage. In 1858 the legal trade of opium was imposed on China. By 1900, 75 million Chinese were addicted to the drug. It took a national revival and 50 years of coercive measures for the country to become opium-free. In the 1920s,

the unrestricted commercial availability of cocaine and heroin in Egypt resulted in a massive epidemic abuse of these drugs which was also curtailed following restrictive measures. (p. 36)

International Collaboration for Prevention

In the nineteenth century there were a number of organizations, particularly in Europe, that promoted the principles of prevention of alcohol and drug abuse. Among these, the first Congress of the International Council on Alcohol and Addictions (ICAA) was convened in Antwerp, Belgium in 1885. It was then called 'The Antwerp International Meeting against the Abuse of Alcoholic Beverages' and its programme was exclusively devoted to the subject of alcohol abuse. The Second International Meeting against the Abuse of Alcoholic Beverages was held in Zurich in 1887. Professor Auguste Forel of Switzerland, mentioned above as a pioneer in the prevention and treatment of alcoholics, was the President of the Organization Committee for that Congress. The first remark on the seriousness of drug problems made in a large-scale conference was in 1903 in Bremen, Germany at the 9th Congress, when Professor Forel presented a paper on narcotic drugs. He actively pursued his involvement with the work of the Congress and in 1907 he was the President of its Stockholm Meeting during which the International Bureau against Alcoholism was created (ICAA 1985, p. 1). Professor Forel continued his vigorous and untiring work in the prevention and eradication of alcoholism and travelled extensively, particularly in Eastern Europe. He was highly impressed by the Bahá'í teachings on abstinence from alcohol and the consideration of work in the spirit of service as worship. In the early 1920s he became a Bahá'í and actively taught its principles for the betterment of mankind (Mühlschlegel 1978).

Since the turn of the century there have been a number of other eminent figures as well as organizations, national and international in character, that have promoted the cause of prevention.

International cooperation in the field of drug control began in the early part of this century when in 1909 the first attempts to limit

143

the shipping of narcotic drugs were made. International drug treaties concluded between 1912 and 1972 provide the legal basis for the present international drug control system. United Nations' involvement in this field began in 1946 when it assumed the drug control functions and responsibilities formerly carried out by the League of Nations. (UN information, Vienna 1987)

In December 1985, because of the rapid dissemination of drug abuse around the world and its pervasive effect on the mind and life of mankind, the General Assembly of the United Nations passed a resolution strongly urging all Member States to use their political will to combat drug abuse and illicit trafficking. The resolution called for a greater concerted effort to be generated by a higher level of political, cultural, and social awareness of the serious consequences of drug abuse. In addition, it called for an international conference to be held in 1987 in Vienna and the adoption of a comprehensive multi-disciplinary outline of future activities in dealing with this serious worldwide problem (Grant 1986, p. 21). Following that resolution, an interregional conference on drug abuse and illicit trafficking was held by the United Nations Non-Governmental Organizations in September 1986 in Stockholm, Sweden. The Stockholm Conference, under the auspices of the United Nations and in collaboration with the Government of Sweden, submitted important and valuable recommendations as part of its resolution to the United Nations. These recommendations contributed significantly to the deliberation of the representatives of governmental and non-governmental organizations of the world participating in a June 1987 International Conference in Vienna. This conference consisted of two simultaneous meetings: one of government representatives of 138 countries around the world, about half of whom were of ministerial rank; the other, conferences and workshops of delegations of some 200 NGOs of the United Nations. The resolution of the International Conference was submitted to the General Assembly of the United Nations in November 1987 for its deliberation and consideration.

In December 1994, the NGO World Forum on Drug Demand Reduction was held in Bangkok, Thailand under the auspices of the

United Nations International Drug Control Programme (UNDCP) and representatives of NGOs from 112 countries attended. In June 1998, the UN General Assembly's Special Session took place in New York to deliberate on the Fight Against the Illicit Production of Psychotropic Substances. The NGOs held their own meeting during this special session.

The Bahá'í International Community, a non-governmental organization of the United Nations, has been closely collaborating with the United Nations in the prevention and eradication of drug abuse and alcoholism around the world. It was represented at the 1987 United Nations International Conference held in Vienna and presented an official Statement (printed at the end of this book, pp. 148–50). It was also represented at the NGO World Forum in 1994 and the NGOs' parallel conference in 1998. During the World Forum of 1994 the present author made a presentation on Parent Education and Substance Abuse Prevention.

A Proposal

The following recommendations are put forward for the control of drug trafficking and the prevention of substance abuse:

1. The governments of the world, irrespective of cultural, economic and political differences, should adopt as a common goal the curbing of the cultivation, production, and trafficking in narcotic and other drugs. This should be accomplished through the setting of strict laws with full cooperation among nations. Any relaxation or leniency in enforcing these laws would be counter-productive and must be strictly avoided. A drastic reduction in the availability of the abused substances will have the following results:

(i) discouraging new and recurrent drug users from obtaining drugs;
(ii) encouraging drug addicts to seek active treatment and rehabilitation.
(iii) promoting a healthy lifestyle and preservation of physical as well as psychosocial and spiritual well-being.

145

2. Health professionals in all fields, including those involved in alcohol and drug abuse, are well aware of the widespread pain and suffering that characterizes most societies today. To turn the tide on much of this suffering, the World Health Organization (WHO) should call upon its entire worldwide membership and health institutions to accept the challenge of abstention from consumption of alcohol and drugs.

3. An international campaign to educate young and old about the dangerous consequences of drug use and addiction should be implemented through educational systems, the media and religious institutions. People should also be educated about ways and means of coping with life stress and difficulty without resorting to alcohol and drugs. Schools and media have an important role to play in the fight against the use and trafficking of drugs, and exercise a potent influence in providing positive alternatives. However, neither the present system of education nor the media have succeeded in developing an effective programme for prevention. Indeed, in most parts of the world, media advertising has glamorized the use of substances such as alcohol. This is obviously an encouragement to drink.

4. One of the very important factors in a campaign against drug use is the example set by important social figures including statesmen, government leaders, artists, teachers, writers, legislators, sport and movie stars and society's heroes in general. If these individuals, by abstinence from alcohol and drugs, set an example for society, it will be easier to educate people in the prevention of substance abuse.

In conclusion, there is today substantial evidence to suggest that it is not only drug availability but also individual alienation, peer pressure, low self-esteem, poor stress management and lack of spiritual insight into the ultimate purpose of life that are contributing factors to the spread of alcohol and drug dependency. The principal antidote is a discipline and a moral conviction based on reason and faith and the development of a system of values, spiritual in nature and universal in scope. Such is the system described in the teachings of Bahá'u'lláh and exemplified in Bahá'í communities around the world.

Prevention of alcohol and drug abuse is a collective responsibility in which individuals, families, educators, administrators, health professionals and all other elements of society must work together to create an environment which will be conducive to psychosocial well-being, personal growth and spiritual fulfilment, and free from substance abuse and its consequences.

APPENDIX

Bahá'í International Community Statement to the United Nations International Conference on Drug Abuse and Illicit Trafficking

Vienna, Austria, 17–26 June 1987

The Bahá'í world community, comprising Bahá'í communities in some 140 independent nations, and representing a cross-section of humanity of over 2,000 ethnic backgrounds, with a membership of four and a half million children, youth and adults of both sexes, lives by the principles and teachings of Bahá'u'lláh, the Founder of the Bahá'í Faith. One of these teachings stipulates the 'total abstinence from all alcoholic drinks, from opium, and from similar habit-forming drugs.'[1]

It is only natural, therefore, that in its commitment to this interdiction, the Bahá'í International Community has been collaborating wholeheartedly with the United Nations campaign on drug abuse; and it enthusiastically welcomes the present International Conference on Drug Abuse and Illicit Trafficking as a significant step in finding ways of preventing and eradicating the dehumanizing habit of drug and substance abuse.

In the spirit of continuing cooperation, we would like, there-

---

[1] From the Bahá'í Writings.

fore, to offer the following observations.

The pervasive spread of substance abuse is not confined, as we know, to the affluent societies of the Western world. Its alarming signs can now be discerned among the nations of all continents. It is not limited to certain social groups; rather it has penetrated almost all layers of human society. Today, millions of human beings, of all ages and all walks of life, submit their minds to the influence of illicit drugs.

At a time when most of the attention is being directed toward combatting the devastating effect of drug abuse, we welcome the increasing interest in prevention, and call for a greater emphasis to be placed on this dimension of the issue. We also propose that, since the demand for drugs constitutes a major human involvement, the attitude of the individual towards drugs, whether relating to production, traffic or consumption, should receive special consideration.

Behavioural scientists are today in agreement that 'attitudes more than knowledge influence the shaping of certain behaviour'. They note furthermore that attitudes 'are acquired during early education and adopted later as a way of life' and that such 'learned attitudes become values, and the values guide decisions about behaviour'.[2]

In developing preventive and educational programmes, therefore, the role of the spiritual dimension of human reality should receive particular recognition. The spiritual reality has been misunderstood or confused with religious superstitions and fanaticism, and thus is often dismissed as unnecessary. Since, however, in the Bahá'í view, the fundamental basis of divine religions is one, closer collaboration and unity of thought and purpose among the peoples of the world regardless of their religious or ideological affiliations is, in our view, both possible and desirable in promoting the fundamental nobility of man in creation, and in protecting his mind and soul from the adverse effects of illicit substances.

2. Ghadirian, A.-M., *In Search of Nirvana: a New Perspective on Alcohol and Drug Dependency*. George Ronald, Publisher, Oxford, England, 1985, p. 48.

In the Bahá'í teachings man is viewed as 'the supreme Talisman,'[3] created noble. The power of thought constitutes his essential reality. Through this gift, assisted by education, a human being can reveal his full potential in the journey through this world.

Thus the Bahá'í International Community believes that an understanding of the spiritual meaning and purpose of life is one of the fundamental steps in educating mankind for the prevention of drug abuse; and perceives happiness as a natural outcome of man's quest for such a realization in daily life, and not as the product of chemical substances.

Likewise, the Bahá'í writings emphasize the crucial role of home and family in cultivating a sense of security and purpose, and in setting behavioural examples. As the non-medical use of drugs is forbidden to Bahá'ís, by following this commandment, parents serve as effective role models for their children.

In this connection, we would like to underline the powerful influence of role models, whether in the family or in society at large, in any campaign for prevention of drug abuse. The value of important social figures – including government officials, teachers, parents, writers, legislators, artists, health professionals, sport stars, and other celebrities and influential personalities – in setting an example by abstaining from illicit drugs, cannot be overstressed.

Finally, it is the hope of the Bahá'í International Community that the governments of the world, regardless of their cultural, economic and political differences, will, in the present conference, come closer to adopting a common goal in preventing drug abuse, as well as in curbing the cultivation and trafficking of narcotics and other forms of drugs, except for medical use.

---

3. From the Bahá'í Writings.

BIBLIOGRAPHY

'Abdu'l-Bahá. 1995. *Paris Talks, Addresses given by 'Abdu'l-Bahá in Paris 1911 -1912*. 12th ed. London: Bahá'í Publishing Trust.

— 1957. *The Secret of Divine Civilization*. Wilmette, IL: Bahá'í Publishing Trust.

— 1978. *Selections from the Writings of 'Abdu'l-Bahá*. Haifa: Bahá'í World Centre.

— 1981. *Some Answered Questions*. Rev. ed. Wilmette, IL: Bahá'í Publishing Trust.

Alcoholism and Drug Addiction Research Foundation (ARF). 1981. Report of an ARF/WHO Scientific Meeting on Adverse Health and Behavioural Consequences of Cannabis Use, Toronto.

Allen, K. 1994. 'Development of an instrument to identify barriers to treatment for addicted women from their perspective', in *International Journal of the Addictions*, no. 29, pp. 429–444.

Allen, R. P.; McCann, U. D.; Ricaurte, G. A. 1993. 'Persistent effects of 3,4- methylene-dioxymethamphetamine (MDMA, "Ecstasy") on human sleep', in *Sleep*, no. 16, pp. 560–564.

American Psychiatric Association (APA). 1994. *Substance Abuse*. In series: Let's Talk About Mental Illness. Washington, D.C.

'Americans starting to realize danger of alcohol, HHS Reports'. 1987. *Psychiatric News* (15 May), p. 3.

Ananth, J. 1978. 'Side effects in the neonate from psychotropic agents excreted through breast-feeding', in *American Journal of Psychiatry*, vol. 135, no. 7, pp. 801–805.

Anglin, M. D.; Hser, Y.; McGlothlin, W. H. 1987. 'Sex differences in addict carriers', in *American Journal of Drug and Alcohol Abuse*, no. 131, pp. 59–71.

Arehart-Treichel, J. 2006a. 'Alcoholism's genetic roots becoming clearer', in *Psychiatric News (Am)* (6 Oct.), p. 25.

— 2006b. 'Researchers hope boosting receptors can prevent alcoholism', in *Psychiatric News (Am)* (6 Oct.), p. 25.

The Báb. *Selections from the Writings of the Báb*. 1976. Haifa: Bahá'í World Centre.

Bahá'í Prayers: A Selection of Prayers Revealed by Bahá'u'lláh, the Báb, and 'Abdu'l-Bahá. 2002. Wilmette, IL: Bahá'í Publishing Trust.

Bahá'u'lláh. 1976. *Gleanings from the Writings of Bahá'u'lláh*. Trans. Shoghi Effendi. 2nd rev. ed. Wilmette, IL: Bahá'í Publishing Trust.

— 1978. *Tablets of Bahá'u'lláh revealed after the Kitáb-i-Aqdas*. Haifa: Bahá'í World Centre.

— 1980. *The Hidden Words of Bahá'u'lláh*. Wilmette, IL: Bahá'í Publishing Trust.

Bahá'u'lláh and 'Abdu'l-Bahá. 1944. *The Divine Art of Living*. Compiled by Mabel Hyde Paine. Wilmette, IL: Bahá'í Publishing Trust.

— 1976. *Bahá'í World Faith*. Wilmette, IL: Bahá'í Publishing Trust.

Beary, M. D.; Lacey, J. H.; Merry, J. 1986. 'Alcoholism and eating disorders in women of fertile age', in *British Journal of Addiction*, no. 81, pp. 685–689.

Becklake, M. R.; Ghezzo, H; Ernst, P. 2005. 'Childhood predictors of smoking in adolescence – a follow-up study of Montreal school children', in *Canadian Medical Association Journal*, no. 173 (4), pp. 377–379.

Bedi, Rahul. 1992. 'Keeping Manipur drug-free: Indian state's torch-bearing women enforce anti-moonshine laws – with a vengeance', in *Southam News*, quoted in *The Gazette* (Montreal) (24 Feb.), p. 1.

Benazzi, F.; Mazzoli, M. 1991. 'Psychiatric illness associated with "ecstasy"', in *The Lancet*, no. 338, p. 1520.

Brindley, Madeleine. 2006. 'Ireland became the first country in the world to ban smoking in 2004', in *Western Mail* (13 Dec.). From www.icWales.co.uk.

Buchan, V. 1977. 'I'm in terrible trouble', in *Listen Magazine* (Feb.), pp. 12–13.

Castro, Janice, and Associates. 1986. 'Battling the enemy within', in *Time Magazine* (17 Mar.), p. 41.

Chandler, William U. 1986. 'Banishing tobacco', in *World Health Magazine* (June), p. 8.

Chassin, L.; Barrera, M. 1991. 'Substance use and symptomatology among adolescent children of alcoholics', in *Journal of Abnormal Psychology*, no. 100, pp. 449–463.

Clare, Anthony W. 1986. 'Drugs are big business', in *World Health Magazine* (June), p. 18.

Cohen, Allan Y. 1971. 'The journey beyond trips: Alternatives to drug use', in *Journal of Psychedelic Drugs*, vol. 3, no. 2, pp. 16–21.

Cohen, Sidney. 1971. 'A Commentary on "The Ethics of Addiction"', in *American Journal of Psychiatry*, no. 128, pp. 547–550.
— 1975. *Teenage Drinking: The Bottle Babies*, vol. 4, no. 7 (Aug.), p. 1.
— 1976. 'Pharmacology of drugs of abuse', in *Drug Abuse and Alcoholism Newsletter*, vol. 5, no. 6 (July), p. 3. Reprinted with permission.
— 1981a. 'Cannabis: Impact on motivation, Part II', in *Drug Abuse and Alcoholism Newsletter*, vol. X, no. 1 (Jan.), p. 1.
— 1981b. 'The one vehicle accident', in *Drug Abuse and Alcoholism Newsletter*, vol. X, no. 2 (Apr.), p. 1.
— 1981c. 'Gift of the Sun God or the Third Scourge of Mankind', in *Drug Abuse and Alcoholism Newsletter*, vol. X, no. 7 (Sept.), p. 1.
— 1981d. 'Substance abuse: Initiation and perpetuation', in *Drug Abuse and Alcoholism Newsletter*, vol. X, no. 9 (Nov.).
— 1982. 'Pleasure and pain', in *Drug Abuse and Alcoholism Newsletter*, vol. XI, no. 5 (June).

Curran, H. V.; Travill, R. A. 1997. 'Mood and cognitive effect of 3,4- methylenedioxymethamphetamine (MDMA, "ecstasy"): Weekend "high" followed by mid-week low', in *Addiction*, vol. 92, no. 7, pp. 821–831.

D'Agnone, O. A.; Basyk, L. D. 1989. 'Some familial dynamic aspects in drug abusers', in *Medicine and Law*, no. 8, pp. 431–432.

Danesh, H. B. 1986. *Unity: The Creative Foundation of Peace*. Ottawa: Bahá'í Studies.

'Demon drink'. 1986. *World Health Magazine* (June), p. 12.

De Ropp, Robert S. 1976. *Drugs and the Mind*. New York: Delacorte Press/Seymour Lawrence.

'Drinking as a way of life'. 1978. *Time Magazine* (22 May), p. 38.

Dobbie, Judy. 1977. 'Substance abuse among the elderly', in *Addictions* (Fall).

Domestic Council Drug Abuse Task Force. 1975. *White Paper on Drug*

Abuse, A Report to the President from the Domestic Council Drug Abuse Task Force (Sept.), pp. 1–9.

DuPont, R. L. 1981. 'Learning from the past to cope with the future', in Nahas and Frick II, p. 268.

— 1984. *Getting Tough on Gateway Drugs.* Washington, D.C.: American Psychiatric Press.

— 1997. *The Selfish Brain – Learning from Addiction.* Washington, D.C.: American Psychiatric Press.

European Collaborative Study. 2006. 'The mother-to-child HIV transmission epidemic in Europe: evolving in the East and established in the West', in *AIDS*, vol. 20, no. 10 (June), pp. 1419–1427.

European Commission. 1998. *Alcohol Problems in the Family: A Report to the European Union* (Eurocare), pp. 7–28.

Esson, Katherine M. 2004. *The Millenium Development Goals and Tobacco Control: An Opportunity for Global Partnership.* Geneva: WHO.

Fauman, M. A.; Fauman, B. J. 1979. 'Violence associated with phencylidine abuse', in *American Journal of Psychiatry,* no. 136, pp. 1584–1586.

Forel, Auguste H. 1937. *Out of My Life and Work.* New York: W.W. Norton.

Frankl, Victor E. 1967. *The Doctor and the Soul: From Psychotherapy to Logotherapy.* New York: Bentham Books.

— 1975. *Man's Search for Meaning.* New York: Pocket Books.

Ghadirian, A.-M. 1969. 'A tissue culture study of morphine dependence on the mammalian CNS', in *Canadian Psychiatric Association Journal,* vol. 14, pp. 607–615.

— 1979. 'Adolescent alcoholism: Motives and alternatives', in *Journal of Comprehensive Psychiatry,* vol. 20, no. 5 (Sept.–Oct.), pp. 469–474.

— 1987. 'Coping with stress in a changing world', in *Herald of the South,* vol. 10 (Jan.), pp. 34–38.

— 1991 'A Baha'i perspective on drug abuse prevention' in *Bulletin on Narcotics* (Vienna: United Nations), no. 43, pp. 35–40.

— Subak, N.E.; Kovess, V.; Gregoire, G.; Prince, R. 1985. 'Alcohol and drug use among Montreal high school students', in *Proceedings of the 34th International Congress on Alcoholism and Drug Dependence,* pp. 22–24.

Globe Magazine: International Alcohol and Drug Problems. 1998. 'Early drinking said to increase alcoholism risk…'. Issue 2, p. 8 (Institute of Alcohol Studies: St. Ives).

— 1999a. 'Addiction among South African farm workers'. Issue 3.
— 1999b. 'UK tops the drug league'. Issue 4, pp. 2–10.
— 2002. 'Living dangerously: The World Health Report 2002'. Issue 4, p. 3.
— 2004a. 'Alcohol: Our kids' drug of choice. Issue 3 (June) (Global Alcohol Policy Alliance: London).
— 2004b. 'Focus on youth drinking'. Issue 3, pp. 19–21.
— 2006a. 'Launch of Asia Pacific Alcohol Policy Alliance'. Issue 3.
— 2006b. 'World Bank calls for action on youth and alcohol'. Issue 3.

Grant, Marcus. 1986. 'Meeting the threat of drug abuse', in *World Health Magazine* (June), p. 21.

Gregory, Ian. 1968. *Fundamentals of Psychiatry*. Philadelphia: W. B. Saunders.

Griffin, M. L.; Weiss, R. D.; Mirin, J. M.; Lange, U. 1989. 'A comparison of male and female cocaine abusers', in *Archives of General Psychiatry*, vol. 46, no. 2 (Feb.), pp. 122–126.

Hao, Wei. 1993. 'Women and substance abuse in China', in *Women and Substance Abuse: 1993. Country Assessment Report*, pp. 197–203. Geneva: WHO.

Harries, D. P.; De Silva, R. N. 1992. '"Ecstasy" and intracerebral haemorrhage', in *Scottish Medical Journal*, no. 37, pp. 150–152.

Hatterer, Lawrence J. 1980. *The Pleasure Addicts*. South Brunswick and New York: A.S. Barnes and Company; London: Thomas Yoseloff.

Henry, J. A.; Jeffreys, K. J.; Dawling, S. 1992. 'Toxicity and deaths from 3,4- methylenedioxymethamphetamine ("ecstasy")', in *The Lancet*, no. 340, pp. 382–387.

Herrington, B. S. 1980. 'Addicted neonates: A grim portrait', in *Psychiatric News* (4 Apr.), p. 3.

Honnold, Annamarie (comp.). 1986. *Divine Therapy*. Oxford: George Ronald.

'Honour of All'. 1985. Brochure about the film.Williams Lake, B.C.: Alkali Lake Indian Band.

Hurley, D. L. 1991. 'Women, alcohol and incest : An analytical review', in *Journal of Studies on Alcohol*, no. 52, pp. 253–268.

Inaba, Darryl et al. 1977. *Psychoactive: The Physiological Effects of Psychoactive Drugs*. Manual of the film, p. 15. San Francisco: Pyramid Films.

Information Canada. 1972. *Report of the Royal Commission's Inquiry into the Non-Medical Use of Drugs: Treatment*. Ottawa.

— 1973. *Final Report of the Commission of Inquiry into the Non-Medical Use of Drugs*. Ottawa.

International Council on Alcohol and Addictions (ICAA). 1985. *International Council on Alcohol and Addictions News*.

International Labour Office (ILO). 1996. *Management of alcohol- and drug-related issues in the workplace. An ILO code of practice*. Geneva: ILO.

— 2006. 'Coming clean: Drug and alcohol testing in the workplace', in *World of Work Magazine*, no. 57 (Sept.), p. 33–36. www.ilo.org.

Jones, H. B.; Jones, H. C. 1977. *Sensual Drugs: Deprivation and Rehabilitation of the Mind*. Cambridge University Press.

Jordan, Daniel C. 1968. *Becoming Your True Self*. Wilmette IL: Bahá'í Publishing Trust.

— 1970. 'In search of the Supreme Talisman', in *World Order,* vol. 5, no. 1, pp. 12–20.

Kalant, Oriana. 1986. 'The cocaine comeback', in *Canadian Doctor* (Apr.), p. 9.

Kassett, J. A.; Gershon, E. S.; Maxwell, M. E.; Guroff, J. J.; Kazuba, D. M.; Smith, A. L.; Brandt, H. A.; Jimerson, D. C. 1989. 'Psychiatric disorders in the first-degree relatives of probands with bulimia nervosa', in *American Journal of Psychiatry*, no. 146, pp. 1468–1471.

Keeve, J. P. 1984. 'Physicians at risk: Some epidemiologic considerations of alcoholism, drug abuse, and suicide', in *Journal of Occupational Medicine,* vol. 26, no. 7, pp. 503–508.

Kline, N. S. 1977. 'LSD: The latch of disinhibition', in *Psychiatry and Social Science Review,* vol. 1, no. 5 (May), p. 4.

Koenig, H. G.; George, L. K.; Meador, K. G. et al. 1994. 'Religious practices and alcoholism in a southern adult population', in *Hospital and Community Psychiatry*, no. 45, pp. 225–231.

Kosten, T. R.; Rounsaville, B. J.; Kleber, H. D. 1986. 'Ethnic and gender differences among opiate addicts', in *International Journal of the Addictions*, no. 20, pp. 1143–1162.

Kosub, David, 1997. 'Vancouver leads in drug use with HIV', in *The Medical Post* (Canada), 21 Oct., pp. 1 and 52.

Lall, B. M.; Lall, G. R. 1977. 'The marijuana epidemic: Meeting the issue and developing positive alternatives', in F. A. Soper (ed.): *Report of the Second World Congress for the Prevention of Alcoholism and Drug Dependency.* Berrien Springs, Mich.: Michigan University Press.

Lample, Paul. 1999. *Creating a New Mind.* Riviera Beach, Florida: Palabra Publications.

Land, Thomas. 1987. 'WHO's attack on drug abuse begins with physicians', in *The Medical Post* (14 Apr.), p. 30.

Leshner, A. I. 1999. 'Science is revolutionizing our view of addiction – and what to do about it', in *American Journal of Psychiatry* (Jan.), vol. 156, no. 1, p. 1.

Levine, S. V. 1980. Quoted in *Psychiatric News,* American Psychiatric Association (4 Jan.), p. 33.

Ling, George M.; Boutle, Susan. 1979. 'Children and drugs', in *World Health* (June), p. 10.

Maddux, James; Hoppe, Sue K.; Costello, Raymond M. 1986. 'Psychoactive substance use among medical students', in *American Journal of Psychiatry,* vol. 143, no. 2 (Feb.), pp. 187–191.

Mann, Jonathan; Daniel, J. M.; Netter, Thomas.W. (eds.). 1992. *Aids in the World: A Global Report.* Harvard: Harvard University Press.

Mathew, R. J.; Wilson, W. H.; Blazer, D. G.; George, L. K. 1993. 'Psychiatric disorders in adult children of alcoholics: Data from the epidemiological catchment area project', in *American Journal of Psychiatry,* no. 150, pp. 793–800.

McConville, Brigid. 1983. *Women Under the Influence, Alcohol and its Impact.* New York: Schoken Books.

Mecca, A. M. 1978. 'Primary prevention: An avenue we must pursue', in Schecter, Alksne and Kaufman (eds.), *Critical Concern in the Field of Drug Abuse.*

Mellinger, G. D.; Balter, M. B.; Uhlenhuth, M. 1984. 'Prevalence and correlates of long-term regular use of anxiolytics', in *Journal of the American Medical Association,* no. 251, pp. 375–379.

Mühlschlegel, Peter. 1978. *August Forel and the Bahá'í Faith.* Oxford: George Ronald.

Mwenesi, H. A. 1996. 'Rapid assessment of drug abuse in Kenya', in *Bulletin on Narcotics* (Vienna: United Nations), vol. XLVIII, nos. 1 & 2.

Nahas, Gabriel G. 1981. 'A pharmacological classification of drugs of abuse', in *Drug Abuse in the Modern World: A Perspective for the*

Eighties, ed. G. G. Nahas and H. C. Frick II. New York: Pergamon Press.

— 1987. 'Prevention: The only solution', in Steed (ed.): *Report of the Sixth World Congress for the Prevention of Alcoholism and Drug Dependency.*

National Institute on Drug Abuse (NIDA). 1993. 'National household survey on drug abuse: Population estimated, 1993'. Washington, D.C., US Department of Health and Human Services, 1994, in Stein and Cyr, 1997.

NGO World Forum on Drug Demand Reduction. 1994. *Women and Drug Abuse,* p. 10. Bangkok.

Noble, Ernest. 1987. 'Prevention by and for all to make a safer future', in Steed (ed.): *Report of the Sixth World Conference for the Prevention of Alcoholism and Drug Dependency,* pp. 25–26.

Nurnberger Jr., J. I; Bierut, L. J. 2007. 'Seeking the connections: Alcoholism and our genes', in *Scientific America* (Apr.), pp. 46–48.

O'Brien, C. P. 1997. 'Progress in the science of addiction', in *American Journal of Psychiatry* (Sept.), vol. 154, no. 9, p. 1195.

O'Connor, B. 1994. 'Hazards associated with the recreational drug "ecstasy"', in *British Journal of Hospital Medicine,* vol. 52, no. 10, pp. 507–514.

The Pan American Health Organization. 2005. 'Global Tobacco Treaty Enters into Force', in *PAHOtoday* (Apr.). www.paho.org/English/DD/PIN/ptoday12_apr05.htm.

Pardini, D. A.; Plante, T. G.; Sherman, A.; Stump, J. E. 2000. 'Religious faith and spirituality in substance abuse recovery: Determining the mental health benefits', in *Journal of Substance Abuse Treatment,* no. 19, pp. 347–354.

PEDDRO (Prevention Education Drugs, a joint UNESCO/European Commission Programme). 1998. Newsletter. 'Synthetic drugs: A new challenge for prevention'. Issue 1–2 (Feb.). http://www.unesco.org/most/peddro.htm.

Pérez de Cuéllar, Javier. 1985. Address to Spring Session of UN Economic and Social Council, in *UN Chronicle,* vol. 22 (May), pp. 42–45.

Piazza, N. J.; Vrbka, J. L.; Yeager, R. D. 1989. 'Telescoping of alcoholism in women alcoholics', in *International Journal of the Addictions,* no. 24, pp. 19–28.

Player, David A. 1986. 'The big killer', in *World Health Magazine* (June), p. 4.

Power, R. 1996. 'Rapid assessment of drug-injecting situation at Hanoi and Ho Chi Minh City, Viet Nam', in *Bulletin on Narcotics* (Vienna: United Nations), vol. 48, nos. 1 & 2.

Prince, Raymond. 1982. 'Culture, race and alcoholism', in *Annals of the Royal College of Physicians and Surgeons of Canada*, vol. 15, no. 7 (Nov.) pp. 595–599.

Ram Nath, Uma. 1986. 'Smoking in the Third World', in *World Health Magazine* (June), p. 6.

Rohsenow, D. J.; Corbett, R.; Devine, D. 1988. 'Molested as children: A hidden contribution to substance abuse', in *Journal of Substance Abuse Treatment*, vol. 5, no. 2, p. 129.

Sanders, J. M. Jr. 1982. 'Adolescents abusing drugs more often at earlier age', cited in *Psychiatric News*, American Psychiatric Association (17 Dec.), p. 12.

Sartorius, Norman. 1986. 'Putting a higher value on health', in *World Health* (June), pp. 2–3.

Saunders, N. 1993. *E for Ecstasy*. London: Nicholas Saunders.

Schecter, A.; Alksne, H.; Kaufman, E. (eds.). 1978. *Critical Concern in the Field of Drug Abuse*. New York: Marcel Dekker.

Schukit, Marc A. 1995. 'Alcohol dependence in women: Is it really unique?', in *Drug Abuse and Alcoholism Newsletter*, vol. 24, no. 1 (Feb.), pp. 1–4.

Schwartz, Richard H. 1985. 'Frequent marijuana use in adolescence', in *American Family Physician*, vol. 31, no. 1 (Jan.), pp. 201–205.

Scott, Edward M. 1972. *The Adolescent Gap: Research Findings on Drug Using and Non-Drug Using Teens*. Springfield, IL.: C.C. Thomas.

Selassie, S.; Gebre, A. 1996. 'Rapid assessment of drug abuse in Ethiopia', in *Bulletin on Narcotics* (Vienna: United Nations), vol. 48, nos. 1 & 2.

Self, D. 2004. 'Drug dependence and addiction – Neural substrates', in *American Journal of Psychiatry* (Feb.), vol. 161, no. 2, p. 223.

Shoghi Effendi. 1963. *The Advent of Divine Justice*. Wilmette, IL: Bahá'í Publishing Trust.

Smart, R.G. 1976. 'The new drinkers: Teenage use and abuse of alcohol', in *Journal of Addictions*, vol. 23, no. 1 (Spring), p. 10.

Smith, R. M. 1979. 'The long, slow stunting of cigarette sales', in *Business Week* (7 May), p. 40.

Sokol, R. J. 1981. 'Alcohol and abnormal outcome of pregnancy', in *Canadian Medical Association Journal,* vol. 125 (July), pp. 143–148.

Solowij, N.; Hall, W.; Lee, N. 1992. 'Recreational MDMA use in Sydney: A profile of "ecstasy" users in their experience with the drug', in *British Journal of Addiction,* no. 87, pp. 1161–1172.

Steed, Ernest. 1987. *Report of the Sixth World Congress for the Prevention of Alcoholism and Drug Dependency.* Nampa, Idaho: International Commission for Prevention of Alcoholism and Drug Dependency, Pacific Press Publishing Association.

Steele, T. D.; McCann, U. D.; Ricaurte, G. A. 1994. '3,4-methylenedioxy-methamphetamine (MDMA, ecstasy): Pharmacology and toxicology in animals and humans', in *Addiction,* vol. 89, pp. 539–551.

Stein, M. D.; Cyr, M. G. 1997. 'Women and substance abuse', in *Medical Clinics of North America,* vol. 81, no. 4, pp. 979–998.

Stein, R. A.; Strickland, T. L.; Khalsa-Dennison, E.; Andre, K. 1997. 'Gender differences in neuropsychological test performances among cocaine abusers', in *Archives of Clinical Neuropsychology,* no. 12, pp. 410–411.

Stuart Houston. 1986. 'The sociology of cigarette smoking', in *Canadian Medical Association Journal,* vol. 134 (15 Apr.), pp. 878–879.

United Nations (UN). Division of Narcotic Drugs. 1982. *The United Nations and Drug Control.* Vienna.

— 1987. 'Review of drug abuse and measures to reduce the illicit demand for drugs by region', in *Bulletin on Narcotics,* vol. 39 (Jan.–Mar.), pp. 4–5.

— International Drug Control Programme (UNDCP). 1996. 'Amphetamine type stimulants: A global review', in *UNDCP Review,* no. 3.

— 1997. *World Drug Report.* Oxford: Oxford University Press.

— Office of Drugs and Crime (UNDCP). 2005. *World Drug Report 2005.* Vienna: UNODC. Electronic version on www.unodc.org.

— 2006. *World Drug Report 2006.* Vienna: UNODC. Electronic version on www.unodc.org.

Universal House of Justice, Research Department of the. 1991. *Compilation of Compilations,* vol. 2, 1964–1990. Maryborough, Victoria: Bahá'í Publications Australia.

Vaillant, George E. 1983. *The Natural History of Alcoholism.* Cambridge, Mass: Harvard University Press.

— 1985. 'Variety of research on genetic markers for alcoholism now underway in U.S.', in *Psychiatric News* (17 May).

Wansi, E. 1996. 'Rapid assessment of drug abuse in Cameroon', in *Bulletin on Narcotics* (Vienna: United Nations), vol. 48, nos. 1 & 2.

Weiss, S. 2002. 'The story of the alcoholic milk drink in Israel', in *The Globe*, Issue 4, p. 20.

Whitaker-Azmitia, P. M.; Aronson, T. A. ' "Ecstasy" (MDMA)-induced panic', in *American Journal of Psychiatry*, no. 146, p. 119.

Winfield, I.; Gorges, L. K.; Swart, M. et al. 1990. 'Sexual assault and psychiatric disorders among a community sample of women', in *American Journal of Psychiatry*, no. 147, pp. 335–341.

The World Book Encyclopedia. 1979 (Chicago). 'Alcohol', vol. 1, p. 321; 'Tobacco', vol. 19, pp. 240, 243.

World Health Organization (WHO). 1987. Media service feature on the UN International Conference on Drug Abuse and Illicit Trafficking, Vienna, Austria, June 1987.

— 1993. *Women and Substance Abuse: 1993. Country Assessment Report.* Programme on Substance Abuse. Geneva: WHO.

— 1996. *Indigenous Peoples and Substance Abuse Project, Report on Planning Meeting (Phase 2).* Programme on Substance Abuse. Costa Rica: WHO.

— 2002. *World Health Report.* Issue 4.

— 2003. *Western Pacific Regions – Health First.* www.who.int/china/media_centre/speeches.

— 2006a. *HIV/AIDS, Child and Adolescent Health and Development.* www.who.int/child-adolescent-health/hiv.htm.

— 2006b. The Tobacco Atlas, Tobacco Free Initiative.

www.who.int/tobacco/statistics/tobacco_atlas/en/.

Zeitlin, H. 1994. 'Children with alcohol-misusing parents', in *British Medical Bulletin*, no. 50, pp. 139–151.

ABOUT THE AUTHOR

Dr Abdu'l-Missagh Ghadirian is a Professor at McGill University, Faculty of Medicine and an Emeritus Physician of McGill University Health Centre. He is a Fellow of the Royal College of Physicians and Surgeons of Canada and a Distinguished Life Fellow of the American Psychiatric Association. He has done extensive research and published over 100 peer-reviewed articles in scientific journals and about 30 articles in other academic media. He is the author of nine books, including *In Search of Nirvana, Ageing: Challenges and Opportunities* and *Environment and Psychopathology* (edited with the late Professor Heinz Lehmann). Some of his works have been translated and published in English, Spanish, Italian, Portuguese, Persian, Russian, Chinese and French. He served for many years as a consultant on the prevention of alcoholism and drug dependency to the Bahá'í International Community, an international non-governmental organization (NGO). Currently, besides doing scientific research, he also teaches spirituality and ethics in medicine at the Faculty of Medicine, McGill University, Montreal.

LaVergne, TN USA
23 January 2011
213631LV00001B/5/A